# United in Grief

## MONIQUE PATTERSON

Genius
Book Publishing

Los Angeles, California, USA

United in Grief
Copyright © 2020 Monique Patterson

Published By:
Genius Book Publishing
31858 Castaic Road #154
Castaic, CA 91384
GeniusBookPublishing.com

ISBN: 978-1-947521-21-6

200212

# Sometimes

Sometimes I catch a glimpse,
In softened waves of blue,
My child, my heart… when I see a smile
I can't help but think of you.

Sometimes these waves fill oceans.
And feelings sting on every shore,
A collections of each memory
And every way I wish for more.

Sometimes I watch for answers
Because each day I call to you.
I ask for faith and courage
And strength… to help me through.

Sometimes I ask for bravery
Like dolphins in the deep,

Because time moves oh so slowly,
And sometimes the road is steep.

Sometimes I want to scream.
This was not what I had planned.
Why you ever suffered,
A mom can't understand.

Sometimes I hear your laughter
And remember you at play,
But My Child I always miss you.
Not sometimes, but every day.

**—Colleen Ranney**

# Prelude

The 40-minute drive from Griffith to Leeton in South West New South Wales is a treat for the senses. Lush green paddocks filled with rice serve as a water trough for an array of birds, including pelicans. There are uniform rows of oranges, lemons and grapes, and if the wind is blowing in a certain way the sweet yet sickly aroma of all three in unison make the hairs in your nose stand to attention. Large sprinkler systems feed the crops, which flourish year-round thanks to the area's irrigation channels. These wide man-made structures allow water to flow into this once arid part of Australia from a number of dams. At certain times of the year rogue pieces of cotton float down the road like tumbleweed, having escaped from one of the tightly bound bales being transported from farm to factory.

Motorists who regularly drive from Griffith to Leeton become accustomed to the friendly waves from other motorists and the nods of acknowledgement from truck drivers. In these parts the locals—a healthy share of them, at least—still adhere to these Aussie niceties. In the same vein, it's a given that if you should be so unlucky as to break down along Irrigation Way, help will soon come, usually in the form of a friendly farmer armed with a set of jumper leads. Should you find yourself in the unenviable position of having run off the road, you can reasonably expect the offer of a tractor to pull you out of a ditch. You can bet your bottom dollar Mr. Friendly Farmer will have something to say about your situation, and your driving ability may be called into question, but it's all in jest. Helping others is not a thing of the past in the Murrumbidgee Irrigation Area like it is in some more densely populated areas of Australia. The steadfast attitude is you help others and they'll do the same for you if and when you find yourself in a spot of bother. It's an unwritten rule that few break. And it's one that locals hope will not be swayed by the rising tide of unspeakable crimes that plague Australian cities. Because Leeton is safe. Neighbours help neighbours by carrying in a bag of groceries or dropping off a warm meal when someone takes ill. Residents don't think twice about opening the door to a knock in the middle of the night. There's no hesitation, no fear that evil will come to the door. Because that happens in *other places*—in other cities, in other countries. Not Leeton. Not their town. Not now. Not ever. Perhaps in the neighbouring city of Griffith, with its ties to the Calabrian Mafia and the enduring mystery of what became of anti-drugs campaigner Donald Mackay, who messed with the wrong crew.

It's common knowledge he's dead, a fact police have conceded, but his remains have never been found. To this day his death serves as a warning to all to not anger the criminal society known as The Honoured Society, `Ndrangheta or La Famiglia. Bodies weighed down with bricks discovered in the Murrumbidgee River found over the years have proved Mackay was not the only one to make this fateful mistake. Speculation about the underworld's role in Griffith today is fodder for many conversations, but these are conducted behind closed doors. There is a constant current of fear that runs through that city, much like the water that pumps through the irrigation channels to change what was once a dust bowl into a prosperous, agricultural haven. However, the water that runs through the channels is dirty and tainted by mud, much like the river of money flowing through the city.

Leeton, on the other hand, has not been touched by this evil. Instead, another kind of evil found this small corner of paradise.

# Chapter One

After finishing high school, Stephanie Scott found herself in the enviable position of being accepted into the teaching program at Charles Sturt University in Wagga Wagga. Like her father Robert, she had dreamed for years of becoming a teacher, and this was her opportunity to see that dream fulfilled. The city of Wagga Wagga in New South Wales, known affectionately as Wagga to the locals, is about three hours by car away from her hometown of Canowindra, where Stephanie had spent her entire life. Stephanie was someone who could only be described as warm, enthusiastic, and infectious in her likability. When she made the decision to move to Wagga to complete her degree, her friends were simultaneously excited for her and devastated that they would be deprived of her charm and her friendship.

Moving to Wagga also meant being away from the love of her life, Aaron Leeson-Woolley. The two had met in Canowindra. Aaron was a high school athlete who had originally caught the eye of Stephanie's father Robert for his ability on the soccer field. In Aaron, Robert saw sporting prowess, a young man of grace and power who could move the ball down the field like few others. But Stephanie saw so much more. She saw a kind, gentle person with whom she could talk for hours without taking a breath. Not long after first meeting, their relationship blossomed. Stephanie and Aaron went on to work at a local supermarket together, stealing precious moments when crossing paths in the aisles whenever the opportunity presented itself.

So when Stephanie began contemplating moving to university in Wagga, it presented a bit of a crisis in their relationship. As it would have if it had been any other couple. Many young lovers would consider taking a break or ending their relationship when one makes the decision to relocate. Distance can breed discontent, and can put undue pressure on what can often be the fragile state of a relationship between two young people entering the next chapter of their lives. But Stephanie and Aaron bucked this trend. There was never a doubt about their future together.

Stephanie settled quickly into university, making friends wherever she went and spreading her infectious energy and love of life with all. Aaron and Stephanie's connection stayed strong despite the distance. They spoke often and never complained about the long three-hour drive to see each other whenever they could.

Upon completing her degree, Stephanie Scott set out to realise her dream of helping the next generation achieve theirs. When she landed a job as a teacher at Leeton High School, it was a celebration. She was elated to share the news with her family and friends that she had landed a job at Leeton, closer to Wagga than Canowindra, but still close to her family. Her parents were secretly pleased that she wasn't going to be too far afield. They knew that she would be a regular guest at their home for a cup of tea and a biscuit with only a three-and-a-half-hour drive between them. It was also a given that Aaron would move to Leeton with Stephanie. The couple were finally going to have the chance to set up a life together. Aaron knew Stephanie would give any home her own special touches and their garden would be the envy of many. He was able to secure a job at the meatworks in Leeton. And so they went.

As had always been the case, Stephanie quickly became part of the social fabric of both the school and the broader community. Her ability to have a group of typically reserved teenagers in bouts of laughter in her English and Drama classes became the stuff of legend at the school. People often gazed at her in awe, wondering what it was about her that made her so special. She was one of those people who lit up a room. It was as if energy radiated from her and she happily shared it with all those around her through her compassion, empathy and ever-present smile. You couldn't help but like her. The bubbly teacher, who was as attractive as she was kind, was totally unaffected by this fact. She would brush off compliments, pointing to her faults instead. This was a way for Stephanie to make others around her feel comfortable. Another rare quality that Stephanie exuded in spades was her willingness to put others first. She did this in all areas of her life. It came naturally to her and she never wanted praise or anything in return. Seeing the spirit of another soar was reward enough in itself for the young teacher.

The couple quickly made friends in Leeton. Stephanie was showered with invitations to attend social outings and Aaron's laidback nature meant he would be welcomed into any social circle. In April 2014, the couple decided to venture overseas to Thailand for a romantic adventure. When Stephanie's sister Kim found out, she was immediately struck with a pang of jealousy that she wasn't joining them. She had a feeling this was going to be a trip Stephanie would never forget. "I remember sending her a message saying 'I don't know why I'm sending you this but I feel like something really special is going to happen,'" Kim later said. Kim's prediction proved right. Aaron got down on one knee at dinner, momentarily leaving his partner in a state of confusion, and proposed. Stephanie accepted his ring with more than her usual enthusiasm. And Kim genuinely couldn't have been happier if it was she herself who now had a ring on her finger. Her sister's happiness meant the world to her. Stephanie sent her sister a photo. Her smiling face was almost overshadowed by the dazzling ring that now took pride of place on her hand alongside the ring her parents had bought her as a graduation present.

No one would have thought it possible, but in the months that followed the engagement Stephanie was even happier than usual. She delighted in planning—in meticulous detail—the day she would marry her soulmate. Stephanie wanted to use her creative flair to create special touches for the day. She chose terracotta pots to adorn with the names of guests to use as place cards at the reception. And she was keen to address each invitation herself. It was her way of savouring every minute associated with what would be the happiest day of her life. She would find herself daydreaming about her first dance at the reception as Aaron's wife, and picturing sharing the day with her family and friends. Aaron and Stephanie were set to marry on April 11, 2015, the Saturday after Easter.

# Chapter Two

Just as she was with her wedding planning, Stephanie was meticulous in the details she left for the teacher who would be relieving her while she was on her honeymoon. She didn't want the students to miss out on anything or to fall behind in her absence and she wanted the transition for the relief teacher to be as smooth as possible. Aaron and Stephanie were invited to a party in Canowindra on the Saturday of Easter weekend. Stephanie told her fiancé to go without her because she wanted to finalise her notes for the relief teacher. Aaron, knowing he would have weeks of uninterrupted time to spend with his bride to be when he returned on Sunday, didn't argue. He knew Stephanie was fastidious when it came to her work, something he respected her for.

Aaron enjoyed catching up with friends back home in Canowindra and spent the night at his parents' home. He and Stephanie stayed in touch via text messages and said goodnight on the phone about 10.30pm on Saturday night. On Sunday morning, Aaron received a SMS (text) message from Stephanie letting him know she was heading in to school for a few hours to finish up. He got ready, said his goodbyes and ensured his mobile phone was charged so that he could call Stephanie on his way home to Leeton. They had spoken the night before about them heading out to dinner at The Village restaurant when he returned, and he had booked a table just in case.

Oddly, Aaron's calls to Stephanie on the trip home went unanswered. He told himself she had probably been distracted by work and allowed her phone to go flat. He arrived home and was surprised to find neither Stephanie's car nor his bride-to-be there. He once again tried to call her, to no avail. Perhaps she was still at the school, he reasoned, or at a friend's place. He got back in his car and drove around the town. Part of him felt foolish, wondering what that would achieve, but another part of him told him he had to do something. This wasn't typical behaviour for his responsible and loving fiancée. The search proved fruitless, prompting a confused, concerned and anxious Aaron to reluctantly return home. He cancelled the couple's dinner reservation and picked up his phone. He began calling Stephanie's friends, at first thinking he would later feel foolish for doing so when she bounded in the door. As the list of names in his phone began to dry up, however, his heart began to beat faster as fear of the unknown set in.

That night Aaron tossed and turned in bed. He craned his ears every few minutes wondering if the noise he heard was the sound of Stephanie's car pulling in the drive. He stared at the screen of his mobile phone, willing it to ring. He scrolled through photos of the couple together, staring into his fiancée's beautiful brown eyes as if begging her to answer his pleas to hear from her. But the phone didn't ring that night, Stephanie's car didn't pull into the drive and sleep never came for Aaron. When the sun shone through the window the next morning and Stephanie's side of the bed remained cold, Aaron knew he had to contact her family. The sound of panic in their voices was obvious. Their Stephanie would never intentionally worry anyone—let alone the love of her life and soon-to-be husband. Aaron and Stephanie's parents decided they had no choice but to contact the police. They knew something or someone was preventing Stephanie from calling home. Repeated calls to Stephanie's mobile phone initially rung out, but later went straight to the message bank. Stephanie's parents, who like their daughter were positive and always saw the best in others, tried to convince themselves that the beaming bride to be would burst in through the door of the home she shared with Aaron and explain her absence with a story they would all sit around and laugh about for years to come. But their longing glances at the door failed to bring her back. And as the minutes ticked by, the gravity of the situation began to sink in. Hope was replaced with desperation.

# Chapter Three

If you stand on the outskirts of a small town and whisper a secret to no one in particular, it won't take long for news to spread through the streets and into homes. Leeton was one such town, and this was the case in the disappearance of Stephanie Scott.

Aaron contacted numerous friends in search of his fiancée and her family lodged a missing person's report with police. Leeton residents, like others who live in small towns, have a tendency to linger when they get their morning newspaper or a carton of milk, or come across a friend while taking their dog for a walk. There are much less than six degrees of separation in Leeton—especially when it comes to a local school teacher who quickly integrated herself into the fabric of the town's society.

Word-of-mouth ensured their news spread quickly throughout the town and a post on Facebook from Stephanie's brother Stuart quickly gained traction further afield. The post, which urged anyone who had seen Stephanie to contact him, was shared more than 1500 times on the first day alone. Locals were also asked to keep an eye out for Stephanie's car—a red Mazda 3 sedan with the registration BZ-19-CD.

Aaron and Stephanie's friends and family quickly sprang into action, offering to help with the search in any way. A close friend of the bride-to-be contacted the local newspaper, *The Irrigator*, asking for their help. She held back tears as she handed over a photo of her friend, telling the reporter that it just wasn't like Stephanie to go somewhere and not tell anyone where she was going.

The Facebook post was quickly shared thousands of times. Some knew Stephanie, some knew her by reputation and others knew nothing about her, but her kind eyes and beautiful smile, along with the generous words so many shared about her, made her disappearance personal. Stephanie could have been anyone's friend, anyone's sister, anyone's teacher. This immediately struck a chord. This was not your typical drug-addict/wanted-person-goes-missing tale. This was the girl next door. Her disappearance was the stuff of nightmares. No one wanted to believe that something sinister could happen in Leeton. No one wanted to accept that it was no longer safe to leave their doors unlocked, for their children to walk home from a friend's at night. There had to be an explanation. Leeton residents quickly came together to search for the loved school teacher. This was something police endorsed.

"The public are our eyes and ears and any information which could assist would be greatly appreciated," Griffith Local Area Command crime manager Paul Smith said in a public statement. When 48 hours passed and there was no word from Stephanie, police decided to knock on doors in the town to seek answers.

Stephanie's sister Kim posted on her Facebook page that she was headed to Leeton from Perth in Western Australia to join the search. "Righto Stephanie, I'm about to board my flight. I'm expecting good news when I switch my phone on in Sydney. I love you xxx," she wrote.

The family, desperate for answers, asked members of the public to search along roads in the area. Robert and Merrilyn, Stephanie's parents, made a pact to stay strong for their daughter. They needed to keep their wits about them to ensure they left no stone unturned. One theory they considered was that Stephanie may have rolled her car and found herself in one of the district's irrigation channels or creeks. It wouldn't be the first time something like this had happened. In fact, in September 2007, Tanya Rider was found alive eight days after she crashed her car in Maple Valley, Washington in the U.S. She was dehydrated, but her brain function was normal. The Scott family found themselves hoping that this was the case, but then grimacing at the thought of their beautiful daughter stuck in the wreck of a car. The feeling of helplessness was all consuming. In times of crisis like this the brain is at one moment your friend and the next your foe. A possible scenario pops in, but then the logical part of your mind dismisses it and the reel of nightmare possibilities returns.

In the times when they were able to seek clarity, the Scott family did everything they could to ensure Stephanie's face and car were flashed on television screens and plastered on the front pages of newspapers across the country. Their stoic ability to get on with what needed to be done was evident early on—they became towers of strength for each other and their community. It's hard to comprehend how they soldiered on with such composure, when behind closed doors they were surrounded by wedding decorations and plans now on hold.

# Chapter Four

As the news of Stephanie's disappearance spread, theories began to emerge. Sadly, as is always the case, there were some who speculated her fiancé might be involved. It's human nature to have suspicions about those closest to a missing person. As the hours ticked by, Aaron's fears for Stephanie grew. He admitted he didn't know what to think, that so many scenarios were flashing by, but none of them made sense. With dark rings under his eyes and dishevelled hair, Aaron looked directly into the lens of a television camera and begged his bride-to-be to ring him as soon as she found a phone. He didn't waver when asked difficult questions by reporters. *Has she ever done anything like this before, Aaron?* reporters demanded. "No," he replied.

He never once got mad at journalists, even when they were asking personal details about his bride-to-be. He didn't skip a beat when asked if she had accessed her bank account, telling reporters she hadn't. It's not as if Aaron didn't care that people thought he may have been involved, more so he had bigger fish to fry. The only thing he cared about was finding Stephanie. He had nothing to hide and if answering these questions helped in any way to bring him closer to being reunited with her, he would do it.

In those first days after Stephanie disappeared Aaron had a lot of time to ponder how perfect their relationship was. The two had attended the same school at Canowindra and shared a love of sport. Their mutual attraction had blossomed into a relationship at Aaron's 21st birthday party—five years prior to her disappearance. Since that time the two had been inseparable. There was no me or you, there was only us. And neither wanted it any other way. Without her, Aaron felt incomplete. The ache in his heart and the frightening narratives that were on repeat in his head made Aaron long to go back in time. *Why didn't I stay in Leeton? What if I never see her again—how will I go on?* Aaron was comforted by the presence of Stephanie's family and friends. He was amazed at their strength, but not surprised. He knew they were just as worried as he was, but he wondered if anyone could miss her as much as he did. The pain was debilitating, the sadness filling his every waking minute with a darkness that had an icy grip on his heart and refused to release it. In spite of this there was a voice in his head that told him to stay strong. That kind, beautiful voice was Stephanie's. And so he did all he could to soldier on, hoping for a miracle. People were struck by Aaron and his genuineness. He always made a point to thank everyone for their help.

The general consensus from members of the public was that Aaron was as much a victim in this tragedy as Stephanie was. However, most would admit to having a tiny sliver of doubt in their mind at some point on one of two points of contention—either Aaron was involved or Stephanie got cold feet.

Steve Mudd, a journalist at *The Area News*, said he was almost ashamed to say he didn't think much of the bride-to-be's disappearance at first. "It was school holidays, she had a wedding later that week, and being a bit of a cynic I wondered if maybe she was just taking a little time for herself," he said. "There was chatter about it in the newsroom— we speculated about what might have happened—but when the family really came out as concerned and the hours dragged on, it became more and more clear that something sinister had occurred. As a journalist you try to be impartial but in reality a lot of us expect the worst to happen, and when we realised she was actually missing—a pretty young woman from a small country town—the thoughts turned to darker scenarios. I hoped against all hope that it was all some misunderstanding, that she'd appear again a couple of days later and be like 'oh I just took a trip to Melbourne' or something."

The Scott family, who had expressed fears that Stephanie may have been involved in a car accident, began plans to try to bring in a helicopter to conduct a search. Members of the public going about their every day lives saw divers searching irrigation channels, officers on trail bikes searching the parkland and volunteers conducting line searches along roadsides. As time ticked by, Stephanie's family had to consider the possibility that someone had taken her against her will. Stephanie's mother Merrilyn later shared that those first days were the darkest she had ever experienced. As the hours turned into days with no word from Stephanie, the family's positivity began to waver. Fatigue began to kick in. Merrilyn tried to remain strong but found it increasingly difficult because she was unable to eat or sleep. She put on a brave face for the media, but every now and then her fears would escape through her lips. "I think 'today, if we don't find her today'… you can't let yourself think about it but you do," she said.

The next thing the family and police did was to ask members of the public to check any home surveillance cameras they may have for any sign of Stephanie or her car.

As the investigation intensified, so too did the public interest in the case, and journalists and photographers began arriving in the small town in droves. With strict instructions from their editors to get a scoop or a new lead, they caught residents off guard with their in-your-face, get-the-story-at-any-cost approach. They stuck out like sore thumbs with their hurried, blunt demeanours and willingness to throw around insensitive questions like grenades in order to elicit a response. Many of the journalists were hardened from years on the job and, unlike Leeton residents, were not personally invested in Stephanie's life. All they knew was that her disappearance had struck a chord with people across the nation.

The story was the kind of sensationalism these journalists lived for. A young, beautiful bride-to-be with the world at her feet disappears in a small town of little more than 10,000 residents, and they knew that their readers and their viewers were hungry for answers. They wanted to be the ones who provided them.

Then, just like that, there was a breakthrough. Stephanie's red Mazda was discovered in a field on a property at Wamoon, 11 kilometres outside of Leeton. Media outlets instantly flashed aerial photos of Stephanie's car across television screens. It was a pivotal moment and an image that became etched in the minds of so many who had been following the missing person case. The car looked so odd; it was entirely out of place, parked off a trail amongst the grass. Sadly, like so many of the developments in Stephanie's disappearance, the discovery led to more questions than answers. It was obvious the car had not been involved in an accident. But where was Stephanie? Did she drive it there or did someone else, and if that was the case, how did they flee the scene? Was there more than one person involved? What really happened?

Stephanie's family and Aaron were now forced to accept that Stephanie probably didn't leave the car there of her own accord. Instead of bringing them closer to Stephanie, it was becoming clear she was far out of reach.

***

As the news continued to dominate national headlines, one man had a lightbulb moment. Paul Halls recalled witnessing something odd on Easter Sunday. He recalled that at the time he had a feeling that he had just seen something that didn't quite "pass the sniff test."

He saw a man wearing a baseball cap and sunglasses walk up the bank of the channel. This in itself was not odd, it was the fact he was carrying what Paul thought may have been an iPad that caught his attention. Paul wondered if the man was going to use it to take a photo. But when he returned to his vehicle, the man no longer had the device. It wasn't until he heard about Stephanie's disappearance that he contacted police. His gut feeling proved correct. Police were notified and divers began searching the channel. Not long after, they retrieved a laptop, which was later confirmed to be Stephanie's.

Another man revealed he had witnessed a man wearing a backpack and T-shirt walking along Griffith Road towards Leeton on Monday. It wasn't a typical route of choice for people out on a morning walk. Could this be the same man Halls had seen?

The mood in Leeton began to change—concern quickly turned to anger, with residents desperate for answers.

# Chapter Five

Fear and anger quickly turned to outrage when on Thursday, April 9, 2015 Australians woke to a salacious front page article suggesting Stephanie was a runaway bride. Stephanie's smiling face and body draped with a bride-to-be sash was accompanied by the headline "Bride and Seek." It was a callous slap in the face for Aaron, Stephanie's family and their friends. Not only was it a vicious rumour they had repeatedly denied, the story hit just hours after police announced they had charged a man with Stephanie's murder. Police had established that the last known whereabouts of Stephanie was Leeton High School. Officers were told to find out whether anyone else had been at the school that day, whether anyone would have been able to access the property out of hours. The school's deputy principal recalled seeing one of the school's cleaners there on Easter Friday. It was not a scheduled work day for the cleaner. Police set about finding out who this cleaner was. Had he returned to the school on the Sunday? Another Leeton resident remembered seeing a white older model ute (utility vehicle) parked at the school on Easter Sunday. Police quickly established that Vincent Stanford, who had worked at the school since October, drove a Toyota Hilux midsize pickup. Armed with these two pieces of information, police decided to interview Vincent and quiz him about his movements over that weekend.

Detective Sergeant Tim Clark of the Griffith Local Area Command sent a plainclothes officer to speak to Vincent. Few people knew Vincent by name as he liked to keep to himself. He would be seen walking through the streets of Leeton with his head down and a *I want to be left alone* look plastered on his face. He would go to the supermarket with his mother on a regular basis, but few ever heard a word uttered from his mouth. The

Stanford family had moved from Zoetermeer in Holland into a modest rental in Leeton after moving to Australia about a year before. He had moved into the area with his mother Anneke and his older brother Luke to be closer to Vincent's identical twin Marcus, who was already living in South Australia.

Vincent was excited about the move. He had two meaningful relationships in his life—the first was with his mother and the second with his twin. Vincent didn't have much in common with his older brother Luke, but the twins shared a love of video gaming, and Vincent was sure the move would be his ticket to turning his passion for gaming into a career. He loved online gaming, spending hours on end playing military-themed games and identifying himself as the Aztec serpent-god Quetzalcoatl. Vincent had always been somewhat detached from the world and had no real desire to make friends—instead enjoying the anonymity and freedom his favourite pastime offered.

Despite his efforts, Vincent was still facing brick walls in his bid to turn his love of gaming into a career. He was obsessed with the fantasy worlds that would allow him to live out his secret desires without judgement and he had an inflated ego regarding his abilities as a gamer. He expected Australia—the lucky country—to offer him his chance to land his dream job—a job in which he didn't have to interact with others. Instead, he was forced to accept work as a cleaner. It was a role he had performed before in Zoetermeer. He didn't love it but he did like the satisfaction the end results afforded him, and he relished the fact that it didn't require him to interact with people on a regular basis. This was something that didn't go unnoticed by students and teachers at Leeton High School. Many later said he never spoke and rarely looked anyone in the eye.

When interviewed at his home, Vincent told the police he had been at the school on the weekend, "cleaning the bins and stuff," but he claimed he had not seen Stephanie while at the school. "Hey, good luck with the search," Vincent called out to police as they left his home. When Detective Sergeant Clark read the cleaner's statement later that day, his gut told him something wasn't right. Vincent had told the constable he had gone to the Golden Apple Superstore on Yanco Road. Luckily, the detective's local knowledge set off an alarm in his head and he was quickly able to determine the shop was in fact closed at the time Vincent claimed he was there.

Vincent was again quizzed about the timeline of events and he again claimed he had been at the store. This discrepancy confirmed police suspicions that the cleaner was lying about where he was on the day Stephanie disappeared. There weren't many good reasons for him to stick so steadfastly to that story.

At about 6pm that same day, two officers returned to Vincent's Maiden Avenue home to ask him to accompany them to the Leeton police station. He was not home, but his mother gave the officers permission to search the premises. It was then they found a set of keys to Leeton High School.

Vincent returned home about 7.30pm. The presence of the police vehicles in the front of the property didn't deter him from entering. Vincent informed the police he had been out taking photos and produced his camera without argument. The hardened police officers were not prepared for that they saw. There among the dozens of seemingly innocuous photos of popular spots around the area were two that would haunt them for years to come. The photos were of a body burnt beyond recognition. When the officers regained their composure they asked Vincent through gritted teeth about the images. Vincent's ridiculous answer, delivered in his monotone voice, sent a wave of anger through the officers. They looked at each other, wondering whether Vincent was stupid, whether he thought they were stupid, or if he was not the full quid. "Downloaded them from a horror movie," he told them.

The officers didn't have to look too far to find more items linking Vincent to Stephanie's murder. A red bra was discovered in his bedroom, along with a bootliner from a car. Like many killers before him, Vincent had kept the items as trophies.

# Chapter Six

Police took little time before confirming to the public and the media that a Leeton resident had been charged with Stephanie's murder. Anyone working at the telephone exchange would have seen lines in and out of Leeton light up in the seconds after that revelation. *Who could it be?* friends asked each other. *Maybe that lad that did time for…* others would surmise. The town was abuzz with speculation, for a good few minutes at least. After that, the gravity of the news sunk in.

Leeton was home to a murderer.

Stephanie Scott was never coming home.

Aaron Leeson-Woolley would never marry his sweetheart.

Leeton would never be the same again. The young teacher had selflessly spent Easter Sunday preparing lesson plans ahead of her planned absence from school. She had taken time out from finalising plans for her wedding—scheduled for six days later—to do what she always did: help another. Sadly it would be the last time the world would benefit from her generosity, the last time it would witness her effervescent smile.

When word got out about the identity of the killer, locals were skeptical. Upon hearing the name Vincent Stanford, it was met with confused looks or shakes of the head. *"Who?"* The news spread like a rapid wildfire throughout Australia. *What a sick, sad world we live in* lamented many. People who had never met Stephanie found themselves breaking down, overcome by emotion. As a way to cope, to convince themselves they were still safe in Leeton, many had pictured a fairy tale ending to the whole ordeal. Stephanie would miraculously be found alive just in time to walk down the aisle and marry the man of her dreams. Or she would be found hurt from a car accident—but go on to make a full recovery and the wedding would be delayed until she was. The reality was far darker.

Leeton residents didn't want to accept that a murderer had been walking among them. The rumour mill shifted into a new gear, with word on the street that a range of Stephanie's personal possessions had been found at the home of the man accused with her murder. And just when Leeton residents thought their pain and anguish couldn't get any worse, it was reported that among the items discovered was a photo of what was believed to be the burnt remains of the missing teacher. This piece of information was rubbished by many. If you brought it up to those in the know, they would simply dismiss it as a fanciful tale weaved by the headline-seeking journalists sniffing around.

It didn't take long for members of the media pack to learn that the little-known killer was set to face court in Griffith. This prompted a mass exodus of journalists and photographers from Leeton to Griffith. Each and every media outlet gave their staff strict orders to do whatever it took to get the first photo of the "Monster of Leeton." Editors would turn a blind eye to photographers standing on the roof of a car or jostling for position with other snappers if they delivered an exclusive image. Instead, for reasons that were never divulged, Vincent was taken straight into custody after a brief hearing in which the accused did not apply for bail. For a few hours—at least—Leeton residents were left alone with their thoughts. The media circus had temporarily relocated, but they would return. And when they did they would be hungrier than ever for the next chapter of their story. Locals felt numb. They felt angry. They felt sad. They wanted answers. They felt as if they needed to do something—but what? They felt like screaming at the sky: *This doesn't happen in our town, not Leeton.*

Thoughts quickly turned to the state of mind of the students at Leeton High School. How would they come to terms with the loss of Stephanie, let alone the fact that she had been killed by a monster who had walked the same halls they did, day in, day out? People who lived in the same street as Vincent, Maiden Avenue, felt like they were part of a horror movie. They wondered if they had ever been in danger, went over encounters with Vincent in their heads, scanning their memories for signs that he was capable of murder. Students spoke about what they thought Stephanie would do in a time like this. They knew she would want to help others to deal with their pain in any way she could. So, in a show of love and respect for their teacher, students began to place cards, ribbons, flowers, teddy bears and candles along the fenceline at Leeton High School. Most chose yellow items—an ode to Stephanie's favourite colour. As the monument grew, droves of people went to the school and sat or stood near the fence weeping. Some hung their heads and consoled others who were unable to contain their emotions. It was a heavy burden for these youngsters who had found a kindred spirit, a mentor, in Stephanie. She had made them think they could do anything they put their minds to. She had made them believe in miracles. What were they supposed to believe now?

In the brief moments when those assembled were able to speak without their voices wavering, they described their teacher as a gem, as someone who was bright and sparkly.

Journalist Steve Mudd said that while he half-expected Stephanie had met with foul play, the news still came as a shock. "That sort of thing just doesn't happen," Mr Mudd said. "I mean, of course it does, sadly, but you don't really think it will happen in your backyard. And that was just the initial reaction; in the days that followed we came to learn things about the murder that were truly horrific— real horror movie stuff—and it just made me feel sick. How on earth does that sort of thing happen to anyone, let alone a bride-to-be? That was maybe the worst thing about it all, the cruelty of the killing just days before what would have been the happiest day of her life. There was a real sense that something had been stolen not just from Steph and Aaron, but also their families, friends and the wider community."

Leeton's Brad McKinnon, who worked with Stephanie's fiancé Aaron at the town's abattoir, launched a fundraising appeal for the Scott family. As the minutes ticked by, the dollars rolled in at a rapid rate. After just three hours the tally hit $3,000. Residents were quick to support the cause because it allowed them to do something positive, to somehow try to counter the evil that had hidden in plain sight in their town.

When someone dies it's often said no one has a bad word to say about them. But this was truly the case for Stephanie in life and death. Many struggled to put into words how they felt about her. It was as if there were no words in the English language that could properly describe the woman who had dedicated her life to preparing the next generation of leaders.

A night-time vigil was organised at the school to honour the slain teacher. At one point, a hush fell over the crowd and many of those assembled looked as if they had seen a ghost. In a spontaneous gesture, a path was created for Aaron Leeson-Woolley and Stephanie's parents, who had come to witness the growing tribute to their fiancée and daughter in person. There were few dry eyes that night—and many said there were none after Aaron broke down as he crouched to read some of the heartfelt messages left for his fiancée. How Aaron and Stephanie's family remained so calm, so measured is something no one will ever know. It was as if they were channelling all their emotions—anger included—into doing whatever they could to honour their beloved partner and daughter.

School was out due to the Easter holidays but this scheduled absence from the institution did not keep many away the night of the vigil. People young and old struggled to comprehend how evil had come to their town and taken such a vibrant, kind young woman who had her whole life ahead of her. Students touched by Stephanie's kindness knew that school would never be the same again. The halls would be quieter with the absence of her laughter, drama would never be the same without her fun-filled lessons, and many would be haunted by flashbacks of how they had looked Vincent Stanford in the eye, not knowing he was capable of such an atrocious act. Some admitted they were in a state of denial; others simply said they didn't know how to feel.

One student, Paris Jennings, said Stephanie had been gushing about her impending nuptials before the school holidays. "She told us she couldn't wait for her wedding day, she was so excited," Paris said. The suggestion that Stephanie might have been suffering from cold feet had been upsetting, she added. "She's not like that," she said.

"She made learning fun. She was not afraid to 'make a fool of [herself]' in drama games," one student gushed. "She was like your best friend," said another. The charming bride-to-be was more than just a teacher, one said. "She was my favourite teacher and she was like family," shared another.

Grace Green lamented that school would never be the same without her favourite teacher's "love and laughter. Ms Scott always knew how to brighten a day," she said.

Stephanie's presence at Leeton High School was a breath of fresh air, according to Adam Mitchell, who was in year 11 at Leeton High School when he spoke to whimn.com. au. "She wasn't just a teacher, she was so much more than that," he said. "Her drama class was more than just another class in the school. She was only 10 years older than us but she was able to bridge that gap. I think fun is an understatement in terms of who she was."

Adam added that Stephanie taught all her students a great life lesson. "If you see someone down, you don't walk away from it," he said. He recalled how Stephanie had reached out to him after a class when a fellow student was making digs at him. "It was the last period of the day and I walked out of the class a bit frustrated and annoyed and down," he said. "She ran after me and said 'Adam, Adam,' and persisted until I stopped and spoke to her about it. You can always spare time to be nice to someone, that's her defining message to me."

Adam continued by saying that students always knew they could talk to Stephanie if they were feeling down. He said she created "a type of fraternity, like a family, like a brotherhood of people that were close and it made it so much closer again." He said she created special bonds with everyone she met and her classroom was a place of no judgement.

"She didn't just tell us what to do and sit on the side and mark tests, she'd get involved and she'd get the people who weren't as confident to feel confident and get really engaged in it all. She was just able to relate with children and she made it fun. Some lessons she could tell that the energy in the room was down and instead of making us sit down and do theory... she knew that it was more important to have a moment in the day where we could sit around and talk and play games. She let us all have a moment to express ourselves, to have a release so we could continue on with our day."

Adam later said that students struggled to come to terms with Stephanie's death when they returned to school. "Most people would like to say that we dealt well with it, but I don't think you can ever deal well with having your teacher taken in the fashion she was," he said. "We definitely banded together and if we knew someone wasn't okay we spoke to each other. We said let's honour her memory by being there for one another—really being friendly and nice to each other—letting her memory and her spirit and honour live on through each of us." Adam also said Stephanie was one of a kind. "She was a caring, gentle, dedicated and relatable teacher. She always ensured her students were happy and never let them leave the classroom unless they were smiling."

Adam said he never imagined something so sinister could happen in the small town he grew up in. He said everyone knew each other and parents didn't think twice about letting their kids play outside. That's why he didn't believe anything untoward had happened to Stephanie at first. "I remember thinking it couldn't be real, that something like that couldn't happen to her and not in our town."

Adam shared that he thought of Stephanie regularly and often played the song she was supposed to dance to at her wedding, Home by Edward Sharpe and the Magnetic Zeros. "She was so excited to be married," he said. "You could tell it meant the world to her."

Adam added that he wanted to honour Stephanie by being as kind and caring as she was. "She had a smile and warmth about her that would light up a room and change anyone's mood," he said. "She cared about the students she taught and she had such a giving nature. She always ensured her kids would laugh. I honestly aspire to care for people the same way she did."

Adam said the heart of Leeton and its residents was still aching. "I think it's made everyone really question the little things we previously took for granted," he said. "The town had its innocence taken away from it in the most horrible of ways."

The news of Vincent Stanford's arrest not only terrified the residents of Leeton, it left them wondering how this had happened and why. Their town had been thrown into the national spotlight for all the wrong reasons.

A former Leeton resident, Joshua Lang, said Leeton was known for many wonderful things, including being a provider of some of the best rice and oranges to the nation. "Now it will be remembered as a town where the community was robbed of a dedicated young teacher, a family of their daughter and sister, and Aaron Leeson-Woolley of the beautiful young woman he was going to marry," he said.

In the next sentence he uttered, he summed up what everyone was thinking. "Myself, the Leeton shire and all those connected with this tragedy are left to ask—why?"

Stephanie's murder came as a shock to many, who were unable to pinpoint why they were experiencing such a rollercoaster of emotions: anger, sadness, relief their loved ones had been spared, guilt for allowing that thought to linger in their mind. Liam Warren, who grew up in Leeton, shed further light on how residents were feeling. He said he had not once been apprehensive about being out late at night in his hometown. It was as if Leeton residents felt as though they had been gifted with some sort of invisible security blanket in their town. Now that blanket had been ripped from their shoulders and the icy cold that clung to their bones for the first time ever was palpable.

Mr Warren knew Aaron through cricket and even though he didn't know Stephanie, he said he had been skeptical about the initial reports saying Stephanie was a runaway bride. However, he thought there would be some other simple explanation. Like many others his mind would not initially allow him to think that his hometown had been harbouring a killer.

This was without a doubt the hardest pill to swallow for Leeton residents. It's one of those things you wish you could sweep under the carpet, pretend it didn't happen for the sake of the town. But then what of Stephanie's memory?

# Chapter Seven

Police next turned their attention to recovering Stephanie's body. A number of locations were searched by officers who had drawn a short straw. This was the type of search that can have no good outcome, but they knew they needed to bring Stephanie's body home to her family. It was the least they could do to help bring some sort of closure to the nightmarish chapter of their lives that would come to be like a scab that forms on a child's knee after a fall. At first it aches, it bleeds and throbs. Then it begins to heal, and just when you think it's about to disappear, a simple bump or knock busts it open again and the pain is just as bad as it was on day one. The police told the public they had a wide geographic area to search, and that they were using phone towers to track Vincent's movements on that fateful day. but they didn't say much more. The public could only guess that Vincent was being evasive in some way, because otherwise he would have led them straight to the body.

Police also gained two unlikely allies who helped them narrow down potential locations. Anneke Noort and Luke Stanford spoke at length with police about their suspicions about their son and brother. Despite their willingness to help, people on the street couldn't help but speculate about whether the family knew or, even worse, had somehow been involved in the atrocious act before, during or after the fact.

Many residents lamented that the tragedy that had changed their town forever was constantly in their thoughts. The range of emotions they experienced made completing seemingly mundane tasks seem almost impossible. They felt sad that the life of a beautiful young woman had been cut short. Sad that her family would never see her marry the man of her dreams. Sad that her fiancé would never experience the joy of welcoming children with his bride-to-be. They also felt angry that evil had chosen their town to carry out its dark desires. And they felt confused about their own deep-seated emotions in relation to Stephanie's death, despite many not knowing her on a personal level. They felt guilty that they were struggling to cope, given the way Stephanie's own family had conducted itself throughout the horrific ordeal. They felt as if they had no right to feel this way. But of course they did.

Stephanie's sister Kim posted an emotional statement on Facebook. "You may no longer be here, but the beautiful memory of you will forever live on," she wrote. "Thank you for 26 unforgettable years, Stephanie. Our lives will never be the same without you."

Stephanie's other sister Robyn posted a photo of Stephanie holding a water pistol in a backyard water fight. It was a powerful image of the teacher, who was a consummate professional by day, helping to guide the community's future leaders, and a loveable larger-than-life character outside of school. "Always and forever in our hearts," Robyn wrote. "That he can't take away from us. That's ours to keep forever and always."

Stephanie's body would be recovered in the early hours of what was supposed to be her wedding day. Stephanie's parents should have been celebrating the impending nuptials of their daughter on Friday, April 10. Instead, they received the call that corroborated what everyone already assumed.

The charred remains of the school teacher had been discovered by the police in one of the area's most well-trodden national parks. Cocoparra, about 70 kilometres from Leeton, is popular among locals and visitors alike with its tracks that take in all manner of flora and fauna and picturesque waterfalls. The detail that many feared—that Stephanie's body had been burnt—was also substantiated. Crime scene investigators were brought in to remove the body and secure the site. It became clear that the Stanford family had camped at the national park before. Perhaps Stanford's familiarity with the terrain was behind his decision to take Stephanie's remains there.

This shocking news was shared with the thousands of people on a Facebook page that would change its name to Rest In Peace

Stephanie Scott. "I am deeply saddened to announce that Stephanie Scott's body has been found in Cocoparra National Park," the post read. "Today is a dark day for Australia. We will always love you Stephanie. You're now our angel from above—please guide us to make the right decisions. You were a beautiful woman, with such potential and an amazing smile. You brought joy to us in the school and in the town. You only tried to do the right thing by your students. You're such an amazing woman and you will not be forgotten."

Perhaps the most heartbreaking of all the Facebook posts was a single photo shared by Aaron Leeson-Woolley. Stephanie was standing with her back to the camera, her wet long brown hair flowing down the back of a dressing gown embroidered with the words "Soon to be Mrs."

By 10pm that night journalists from media outlets staying in Leeton to cover the case had converged at the national park where Stephanie's body had been found. The site was roped off with police tape, but those at the scene could see the forensic team members, dressed in white, ducking in and out of the darkness to the place where Stephanie lay.

A State Emergency Service truck and a van with floodlights were parked near the side of the gravel road. The eerie quiet of the still night and the starlit sky was in direct contrast to the horrific event that had brought those assembled to the national park that night.

In addition to the occasional whispers shared by journalists and photographers was the sound of the motors of the assembled taxis, an odd addition to a crime scene but a necessity for the journalists who had been attempting to numb their own emotions about the case with alcohol. Two local journalists raised their eyebrows at each other, wondering how the visitors would explain the fares to their bosses between the taxis that stayed at the site for hours and driving 70 kilometres to the scene from Leeton. But they knew that the alternative—telling their editor or producer they hadn't attended because they weren't sober enough to drive—would have been a far greater problem.

The scene that night was sobering. No one showed any signs of being intoxicated.

The journalists stood in silence for the most part. A few head nods were exchanged, whispers between colleagues. But aside from that the only sound that could be heard was the rustling of the full body suits the forensic services officers were wearing as they went to and from the area where the grisly discovery had been made. Midnight passed, meaning that Stephanie's body would be removed from the forest in the early morning hours of her wedding day. That fact was not lost on anybody. Some felt sick to their stomach that they had complained about their workload and the state of their accommodations in Leeton. The news crews assembled were torn about what they were expected to deliver from the site that had become a crime scene, and about what could they do to ease the pain of the family who would wake the next day—the day their daughter was set to be married—to grisly details about the discovery of her burnt body. This would haunt many for years to come.

One journalist found it difficult to sleep for months afterward and could hardly listen to others complain about day-to-day issues. "I was at work and my colleagues were complaining about minor things. I found myself angry they were concerned about such minor things when a family was grappling with the realisation their beautiful girl had been violated and killed. I also felt guilty, as if I was not entitled to feel such emotions. I had never met Stephanie so why was I feeling so emotional—surely that was selfish."

Everything seemed insignificant and her usual patience and empathy towards others was replaced with frustration and sadness. The journalist, who did not want to be named, said she experienced a rollercoaster of emotions covering the story. "It was without a doubt the hardest story I've ever had to cover," she said. "I've had nightmares, many sleepless nights and I eventually had a full-blown nervous breakdown."

The journalist said that after months and months of sleepless nights thinking about Stephanie, she felt like her brain snapped. "I don't know what happened but I became all paranoid," she said. "For some reason I felt like I knew too much about her death and I started to think someone was out to get me. I had to seek medical assistance and realise the thoughts I was having were illogical. I think it was my brain's way of telling me to slow down, to stop obsessing about the case and how unfair it was. I knew if I didn't, I would become bitter and would stop seeing any good in the world. I'm OK now but, as I said, I think of Stephanie often."

The journalist added that it had been difficult to watch the Scott family file in and out of court time after time—often with very little outcome, just an adjournment to another day.

There was also the pressure to deliver stories on Stephanie's death and criticism when another publication had a scoop, the journalist shared. "We all felt so horrible, intruding in the lives of Stephanie's family and fiancé," she said. It was a juggling act trying to meet the expectations of managers to cover the story, yet do so in a sensitive way. In fact, she felt her future with the company was under threat because she had not set up camp on the front lawn of the Scott family or hounded Aaron to share his thoughts. "Often people have this perception about journalists—that we're all cut-throat, that we somehow thrive on this type of thing. Well, we don't. I have a younger sister who is a teacher and to this day I get anxiety when I know she is going into her work on a weekend. Perhaps there are journalists somewhere in the world who don't have a problem picking up a phone or knocking on a door and asking grieving people personal details about their loved one, but I've worked in the industry for more than 15 years and I've never met one. We're not monsters, for God's sake, we're people too. And I, for one, was deeply affected by Stephanie's death. I still am to this day. The chilling details haunt me and I believe they will forever. I shudder to think about the effect it has had on Stephanie's family, fiancé and friends."

The journalist shared that she still thinks often about Stephanie. "I have no doubt she would have been a mother by now. By all accounts she would have been a great mother. The fact her chance to experience the joy of motherhood, which I have, was stolen from her is one of life's greatest injustices. It makes me sick."

***

About 2.30am at Cocoparra National Park on April 11 a white Ford station wagon drove down the usually deserted road towards the national park. Anyone who passed the three men in the vehicle could easily have thought they were mates headed home after a few hard-earned drinks following a busy work week, but in fact they had been tasked with the job of transporting the burnt body of a young woman to the morgue. The men in the vehicle emerged less than half an hour later with the body of the beloved teacher in the back of their car.

Journalist Steve Mudd said he would never forget that night. "It was cold, the sort of special cold you get out West after Easter where every last bit of warmth struggles to touch you. It was a pretty clear night and the moon was fairly full."

Mr Mudd said he received a late call from his editor that night—between 10 and 11pm.

"We were going to go out in [my editor's] car but my wife and I had just bought a little Toyota RAV4 and I suggested we might need it if we had to go off-road. [My editor] had Google Maps or something on her phone and we made our way out to the park—I don't know if she'd ever been there before but I certainly hadn't—and we sort of blindly followed these trails until we saw some police at a farmgate."

Mr Mudd added that that the two kept going around a bend until they saw the road lit up with floodlights from a big truck. "The media pack was maybe 50 metres down the road behind the police tape and we just pulled up and got out. We both had cameras with us. I cranked mine right up to maximum sensitivity so we could at least get a grainy shot if need be. But I didn't even stop to think about what I might be trying to take photos of."

Mr Mudd shared that knowing what he knew now, it was obvious why the media was kept at a distance. "We got some shots of the cops doing their thing, people walking about up the road."

Mr Mudd said after a few hours... "we decided to bail out as there was no indication how long that might go on for and whether we'd get anything—especially since it was so cold and by then well after midnight."

As the two drove towards the police they had seen at the farmgate, he slowed down and rolled down the window, asking what was going on. "The sergeant I spoke to asked if we were local media and I said we were." The police officer told the pair to "pull up down there a little way and wait five minutes. Sure enough, a few minutes later a station wagon drove into the paddock, then maybe 10 minutes later it came back out." The two could only assume that the body of Stephanie Scott was in the back.

"I remember snapping photos of everything, then later on wondering whether I should have," Mr Mudd said.

He said he and his editor went to their office, posted a story online and went home. "My wife asked about what was happening and I simply told her 'they found her.' I still haven't told her a lot of what we would later learn, because frankly I wish I didn't know either."

*The Area News* sales manager Alan Barton said people couldn't help but speculate about what the police had found. "It seemed to play out like a slow-motion nightmare and the rumour mill went into overdrive about what had happened to Stephanie," Mr Barton said. "I didn't know this at the time, but I found out from a source within the NSW Police Force that they had a suspect almost immediately and that the death was as bad as you could imagine. Of course, subsequent court documents spelled out the course of events in horrific detail."

# Chapter Eight

On what had become perhaps the saddest day of Aaron's life, no one would have thought twice if he had decided to remain behind closed doors, alone with his grief. But it would soon become apparent that Aaron and the Scott family were not like most people. When he pulled himself out of bed that morning and pulled on a yellow polo shirt instead of the suit he had intended to wear on that day, he thought about what his bride-to-be would do if faced with this situation. Stephanie would want to ease the pain of others. She would want to console her loved ones while putting aside her own feelings. So that's what Aaron did. It became his wedding gift to his soulmate.

In an incredible show of strength and as a way of expressing gratitude to the community who had rallied around them, the Scott family invited Leeton residents to join them for a community picnic at Mountford Park that day. Mourners wore yellow—Stephanie's favourite colour.

The family had invited residents the day before via a statement on social media. "Tomorrow [Saturday] should have been the happiest day of Stephanie's and Aaron's lives," the statement read. "To help us all through this difficult time, we invite everyone to join us at Mountford Park, Leeton, tomorrow [Saturday] for a lunchtime affair to celebrate the life of our 'Button-Nose.'" The heart-wrenching statement was posted before Stephanie's body was recovered from the bushland an hour away.

No one would have thought any differently of the family if they decided to stay home after this horrific revelation. But, true to their word, they attended the community picnic and welcomed with open arms all who attended. The family stood united, stoic and determined to ensure the day was about Stephanie.

Her dad Robert Scott addressed the hundreds gathered. "Thanks very much to the people from Leeton and everywhere else today for coming up to this park to have a picnic lunch together to celebrate the life of our beautiful daughter," he said. "It's been most helpful in helping us to have some degree of closure of her life and, as my [other] daughter put on Facebook, unfortunately she was taken away from us for a short time but now we've got her back and we'll restore her dignity and that's most important to her family, and it will also assist those that knew her to deal with this tragedy.

"Stephanie was a bright, witty, intelligent, fun-loving girl and a young woman who obviously has impacted on many people here today. Our wishes for the future are that that will continue in your minds, [that] you remember her as the girl she was and I'm sure, wherever she is now, she would wish that to be the case."

Mr Scott told the crowd that a tragedy had happened and no one could change that. "We can't deal with it any better than we have," he said. "But we do know that we had a great girl and we are going to continue to remember her for what she was."

If you were a visitor driving past the town's picturesque botanic gardens that day you might have glanced at the dozens gathered and wondered whether it was a celebration of sorts—a school reunion perhaps, a sporting team celebrating a win with the release of dozens of yellow balloons. The embraces exchanged could have been typical of myriad events that were cause for celebration, but dark shades covered the red eyes and tear-stained cheeks of those assembled. There was no music playing that day; instead, nature put on its own treat for the slain bride. The sun shone, with speckles of light reflecting off the trees and offering a warm layer of protection, much like an infant's blanket, to the people drowning in grief.

Aaron, flanked by family and friends, struggled to hold back tears. When friends saw him put his head in his hands or cover his mouth to muffle a whimper, they would put a protective hand on his back or shoulder and he would regain his composure.

That day, Stephanie's sister Kim shared a poem on her Facebook page she had intended to read at Stephanie's wedding. "My little sister, Stephanie Clare Scott, is now a wedded wife, believe it or not," she wrote. In the poem she described Aaron as the luckiest man and welcomed him as an honorary member of the Scott clan. *"They met in Canowindra, young and sweet, flirting at IGA, between the creamy pasta salad and cold meat. Stephanie and Aaron made a good team, a match made in heaven, so it would seem. They make each other smile, they can fill a room with love, joking and laughing, they fit each other like a glove. You're beautiful people, when you stand alone, together you're strong, you set the tone. I wish you all the happiness, for the many years to come, may you fill each other with joy and never be glum. I'm sure you'd all agree that their bond is unique, special and happy, their love is what we seek."* The poem made people reflect on the injustice of what had happened. How had someone so young, so good, so kind been taken in such horrific circumstances? And what—if anything—could they do or say to try to somehow help this grieving family?

Once again the residents of Leeton had been thrown into a situation where they experienced a dichotomy of emotions. Sadness, amazement at the incredible strength shown by Aaron and Stephanie's family, anger that one man had tarnished all that was good about their town, and confusion about why this had happened.

Every now and then a smile crept onto the face of one of the people gathered at the park that day. And while no words were spoken, it was clear to all that the smile was at the thought of Stephanie.

Journalist Steve Mudd praised the Scott family. "I really credit the family for inviting the community to join with them in their pain, I think that was a very healing thing," he said.

Mr Scott said his family had been touched by the kind words and support shown by Leeton residents. While shopping at Woolworths he was heartened when people stopped to tell him their memories of his daughter.

In another touching gesture, when he went to pay for his groceries, Mr Scott was told someone had donated $100 to management to pay for his items when they saw Mr Scott at the store. Businesses in the town flooded the Scott family with offers of free accommodation, food, and other items.

When the Scott family and Aaron Leeson-Woolley left Mountford Park that day, they could reflect that Stephanie had gotten her wish. She wanted her wedding day to be about other people and in a sad way it had been.

Elsewhere in Australia other brides paid tribute to the slain teacher. Melbourne bride Kat Abbott, who married her own sweetheart that day, tied yellow ribbons to her bouquet, while television personality Lisa Wilkinson encouraged people attending weddings to wear yellow. "If you're getting married tomorrow or simply attending a wedding as a guest, why not wear a touch of yellow in memory of Stephanie?" she wrote on Instagram. "And if you can, spread the word.... It's the very least this beautiful, committed young teacher deserved."

Facebook profiles around the country turned yellow and former brides posted photos of their wedding dresses in memory of Stephanie under the hashtag #putyourdressout.

Shauna Norman, who previously lived in the Riverina region near Leeton, started a Facebook page Stephanie Scott— Put Your Dress Out as a tribute to the teacher. She said when she heard about Stephanie's disappearance, "I was horrified. I felt Stephanie's fear. I know that would sound bizarre to some, but it was almost overwhelming. Her last moments must have been horrifying. When the news reports kept coming—before Stephanie's lifeless body was found—I was almost willing her to be OK." Ms Norman said Stephanie impacted her in a way she found difficult to describe. "Young, beautiful, about to be married… so trusting and unsuspecting," she said.

The outpouring of emotion gave some comfort to Stephanie's family and friends, who were desperate to put thoughts of the circumstances of her death out of their mind on what should have been a joyous day.

Leeton's soccer team was unable to take to the field that Saturday. Both the bride-to-be and her fiancé Aaron Leeson-Woolley had been heavily involved with the club. President Rod Harrison said Stephanie's death had hit club members hard. "The boys didn't have football on their minds this week, and neither did anyone else at the club." He added that many of the club's players attended the day for Stephanie at Mountford Park. "Saturday was a tough day," he said. "We went off to the park with the rest of the community to give Stephanie a nice farewell and celebrate her life. We just tried to support Aaron's and Stephanie's family as best we could."

Mr Harrison said he had been amazed at how other soccer clubs were honouring the slain teacher. "We've been blown away by the support of clubs in the football community, and not just locally," he said. "All the support is amazing and very appreciated. It won't be forgotten."

Stephanie was also well-known and much loved at a soccer club in Wagga Wagga, the Tolland Wolves. She had played with the club while she was at university and was captain of the team for three years. Her coach Steven

Wait said Stephanie lit up a room when she walked into it. Mr Wait said Stephanie would be remembered as the heart of the club during the time she was a member. Every week Stephanie donned her number 10 jersey and "gave her heart and soul" out on the field, he said. "Steph always finished with a smile, win or lose." Mr Wait said Stephanie's number 10 jersey would be retired.

Ruby Scanlon, who lived in the same on-campus accommodation block as Stephanie at Charles Sturt University in Wagga, said she was shocked by Stephanie's death. She said Stephanie loved music, dancing and the colour yellow. "She was just beautiful, everyone loved her," Miss Scanlon said. "She was really goofy and fun. We all loved her."

The Riverina Lions AFL women's football team wore yellow jumpers in a match against Canberra to honour their former teammate. Julie McLean, assistant coach and captain of the team, said Stephanie would be sadly missed. "Steph was a valued member for us, playing over three different seasons… for the Riverina Lions when she was a university student here," she told ABC news. "So we forged great friendships and have many great memories of her at our club. We wanted to make something positive rather than a sad day so we wanted to honour her. We had a great day just remembering all the good times and plenty of laughs."

"Scotty Day" was attended by Stephanie's family and fiancé. "So just prior to the game, we had both teams merge on the ground and we had a small presentation and presented a number 19 jumper, one of the specially made yellow ones, to Steph's family and fiancé," Ms McLean said. "And we were lucky enough to have Steph's four-year-old nephew Samuel come and do the coin toss for the day."

"Just [with] the jumpers alone we have made over $5000 and we are still counting through gate takings and any donations… so we should get a good amount to go back to the Scotts," Ms McLean said.

Leeton's Michelle Tweedale told Fairfax Media her family was devastated by Stephanie's murder. "My 12-year-old son just hugged me and said 'I don't want to believe it.' She

[Stephanie] was his soccer coach at school and he knew the guy that has been charged," she said. "I have four sons that know her from school and the first thing they said was 'Ms Scott is an amazing and beautiful lady that would help you out no matter what.' Our hearts go out to Aaron and Steph's family, we are all so lost for words at the loss of our beautiful friend and mentor. Our kids strived to be like her and it is a cruel blow to our community."

Courtney Sayer, who met Stephanie while playing soccer in Wagga Wagga in 2009, said she was devastated by the loss of her friend. "I was scrolling through my Facebook feed on the Monday before Steph's wedding and there were reports she was missing and posts from people calling for her to come home," Ms Sayer told *The Maitland Mercury*. "I was actually asleep when mum came in and asked me had I heard the news that Stephanie had been murdered. Steph and I always stayed friends... I'm just so devastated."

Ms Sayer said Stephanie was a kind and caring girl. She said her friend would have been proud of the way everyone had banded together following her death. "I think everyone is just trying to get through this as a community and to support the two families who are struggling most at the moment," Ms Sayer said. "And I think in some way Stephanie would be very proud of the movement this has created and I think she would feel extremely loved. The world has lost a beautiful soul."

A number of Stephanie's students also spoke about their teacher. "She had an infectious laugh, which made the whole class laugh with her," said one. "My first day of drama in her class was one of the most important days in my life," wrote another. "I was inspired and have a love of drama that I want to pursue for my future." Another student said Stephanie went far beyond working a job and getting money for it. "She wanted her students to be inspired."

People across Australia took to social media to express their shock and disbelief over Stephanie's death. "I simply cannot comprehend the grief of Stephanie's family and friends, not to mention the ripple effect it will have on the Riverina towns," Morag Jones from Northcote in Victoria wrote. "I am a past student of Leeton High School and I'm terribly saddened by the events over the past week. I'm sure there will be thousands sharing their love and support to all those grieving."

Chrissie Lorenz from Brisbane thanked Stephanie for being a brave educator. "Your hard work and contribution will be remembered," she said. "My sincerest and heartfelt gratitude to your fiancé and family for sharing such a beautiful individual with us. I'm so sorry for your loss and I know that no words or actions can take away the pain that you must be feeling."

Catherine from the Hunter Valley said the loss of such a positive, intelligent and beautiful woman was beyond words. "I am feeling your pain and bewilderment at such an unbelievable crime," she said. Stephanie "… will not be forgotten. I am very sorry that she was not able to enjoy the lovely life she planned."

Leeton's Faith Kennedy said Stephanie's family and friends were in her thoughts. "Rest in paradise Stephy—was a pleasure to meet such a kind, caring lady."

The police officer in charge of the murder investigation, Griffith Local Area Commander Superintendent Michael Rowan, said people should not be living in fear. He said murders were rare and there was no evidence anyone else was involved.

"This is a particularly harrowing crime," he said. "It's traumatic for everyone involved. But these sorts of crimes are very, very, very rare and you know while people are concerned and all that sort of thing I would hate to think people would change their behaviour other than normal behaviour in terms of self preservation and protection."

But that was easier said than done. Blinds that had gathered dust in homes were now pulled down at dusk, keys were removed from front doormats, deadlocks were bolted, and people slept fitfully in a way they never had before.

As the holidays drew to a close, Leeton High School students had to face the grim reality they would be returning to school with the knowledge Stephanie would never step foot there again. Students were assured there would be plenty of support on offer. "Tomorrow is the start of what will be the most difficult week of school life for both students and teachers," a post on the school's Facebook page read. "We will be aided by a large number of people in supportive roles and there are several individuals and organisations to whom we offer so much gratitude. More importantly though, we have each other. Rest assured if you stumble or fall, you will do so into the safe hands of many who care about you."

Stephanie's sister Robyn commented on the post, sharing a touching message with students. "Just remember what my beautiful sister loved," she wrote. "Teaching all you amazing students and seeing your smiling faces. You are the ones who made her want to be the most amazing teacher, friend and person she could be. Be strong, Leeton. For Steph. And know she will be with you all in spirit as I know she is with her family and friends xxxxxxx."

Despite these reassuring words the students were anxious about returning to the classrooms where they had laughed with Miss Scott, the halls where they had exchanged smiles. They were worried that every part of the school would remind them in some way of their beloved teacher who had become much more that than. She had become a mentor, a friend, a shoulder to cry on, and a sounding board for ideas about their future.

Stephanie's father Robert said he believed his daughter was now in the best place possible. "When you die I don't know what happens really, but you leave this body and our spirit is what goes on," he said. "She had plenty of spirit so, whatever happens, she should be in the best place possible because she had one of the best spirits you've ever come across."

# Chapter Nine

In the days following the discovery of Stephanie's body, the change in Leeton was palpable. In a sense reality had set in. People walking down the street greeted each other in a different way—not with their usual smile and a "morning" or "hey, how you going?" but with a forced half smile and a knowing nod of the head. The line up at the supermarket that once gave residents a few extra minutes to share a conversation with a friend was now a source of great frustration. The town's set of traffic lights seemed to stay on red longer. Husbands and wives bickered over minor things they never would have before. Their grief had pushed them to a breaking point.

When Stephanie disappeared, residents had a purpose. They had kept themselves busy trying to help locate the bride-to-be. After her body was found, shock set in. Now people were left alone with their thoughts and the dark cloud that had set in over Leeton when it was revealed a monster lived amongst them.

Stephanie's family now had the task of planning her funeral. She would be buried at the place she had chosen as her wedding venue—a picturesque function centre in Eugowra. The song that had been chosen to mark the couple's first dance as husband and wife, Keith Urban's *Making Memories of Us*, instead was played as the 26-year-old teacher was buried. The lyrics were almost too much for Stephanie's fiancé to bear. The two had sung it together many times before; *I wanna sleep with your forever, And I wanna die in your arms.* That is something that he had pictured— the two growing old together surrounded by children and grandchildren. The grey sky over the function centre was briefly brightened as dozens of yellow balloons were released. But it was a fleeting moment overshadowed by the total injustice of it all.

Once again the Scott family remained stoic—how they were able to do this to ensure their darling daughter had the send-off she deserved remains a mystery.

Stephanie's sister Robyn said what the whole world was thinking: "The world is far less bright without her in it. Our lives less full and our future less whole. How can this happen to someone so good?"

Stephanie's sister Kim told mourners the beloved teacher had a strong sense of who she was. "Steph never cared what anyone thought of her," Kim said. "She had an easy way about her that meant she could get along with anyone."

In Leeton, businesses closed between 1pm and 2pm as a mark of respect. The usual hustle and bustle of the main street was replaced with an eerie quiet. It mirrored the status of the hearts of residents—closed.

In another unexpected turn of events and one that people didn't quite know how to take, Vincent Stanford's mother Anneke asked Leeton mayor Paul Maytom to pass on her condolences to Stephanie's family. She said she had been suffering from shock and grief since her son was arrested. Mr Maytom said:

"Obviously, she herself is traumatised by this whole incident too. I think it [is] a good thing to let her know we are there for her and give her the opportunity to talk to someone."

After the service, Stephanie's nearest and dearest returned to her hometown of Canowindra to continue to celebrate her short life and the unforgettable stamp she left on the world.

In the days, weeks and months that followed the sombre day, their thoughts would turn to ensuring justice was served. Vincent Stanford had changed Leeton, its residents and its story forever. He had taken one of their best. And for that he had to pay.

The public wanted to know about the man who had made them question everything they knew. The media put on their detective hats and began searching for any snippet of information that may provide a clue, a moment in time, an action that may have led him to snap. Or evidence of a psychopath in the making.

# Chapter Ten

Leeton residents were not alone in their fears. Like many senseless murders before it, Stephanie's death was a constant in the minds of Australian women everywhere. Former Leeton resident Michelle Gordon said it was a sad state of affairs. "What happened to Stephanie Scott is an absolute tragedy. It's sickening, and speaking to women in Leeton I know they are scared. I think self-defence skills are something all women should have."

Natasha Stott-Depoja, who was once Australia's Ambassador for Women and Girls, said in an article for *The Daily Telegraph*, Stephanie's "murder has made us sad and angry. The notion of women as prey is insidious and unbearable, yet our society has seen many such cases this year alone. The frustration and sorrow with which Australians responded to the death of Stephanie Scott have highlighted the growing momentum for change and for the violence to stop."

Ms Stott-Depoja said sexual assault, domestic and family violence were the nation's shame. "Australians are sick of the statistics," she said. "This is our national emergency."

Jacqueline Lunn wrote an article for website Mamamia about Stephanie's death. "There is a reason a woman feels fear," she wrote. "There is a reason fear wins over logic when you are a mother. Men like Stanford are that reason."

It was not the first time Australians had been shocked and deeply saddened by the senseless murder of a beautiful young woman with her whole life ahead of her.

On September 22, 2012, Jill Meagher was out enjoying a drink with friends. After leaving a pub in Brunswick, a suburb of Melbourne in Victoria, the 29-year-old was raped and murdered while walking home. She was killed by a man she didn't know and CCTV footage from a shop Jillian walked past on the night she disappeared showed she was simply in the wrong place at the wrong time. It shows her talking to a man wearing a blue hoodie at around 1.42am. She most likely was simply polite to the man who would ultimately take her life.

The man was Adrian Bayley, who is now serving a life sentence for Jill's murder.

Jill had worked at the ABC and, like Stephanie, "she touched the lives of many," a statement issued by the ABC said. "She was witty, intelligent and great company. Her friends and workmates at the ABC will miss her greatly. The tragic outcome will undoubtedly weigh heavily on them…."

After Jill's death, about 30,000 people marched along Sydney Road in Melbourne as a tribute to the slain journalist. Like Stephanie, Jill left behind a heartbroken partner, her husband Tom Meagher. The grieving husband had, like Aaron Leeson-Woolley, endured suggestions he may have been involved in the days following his wife's death.

In July 2018, Mr Meagher wrote an emotional letter to the slain journalist on what would have been their 10-year wedding anniversary. "Ten years ago today, I was lucky enough to marry this incredible human," Mr Meagher wrote. "When I woke up that day, continuously fumbling over the elusive art of tying a tie and nervously downing cheap white wine way too early in the morning, I imagined the seemingly endless stretch of time we would have together."

Mr Meagher said he pictured what their life together would be like in 5, 10, 20 years. "We never made it," he wrote. "Four years later she was brutally and violently taken from this world."

He said not a second went by when he didn't think of his beautiful bride. "Only five weeks ago I stood in the Wicklow mountains where we were married, looking up at the canopy in the woods behind the grounds, as I have done many times in the six years since her death."

Mr Meagher added that his wife and her killer presented the extremes of good and evil—something Stephanie's family could surely relate to. "The arsehole that took her from this world communicates with us through violence, misogyny, hatred and death," he wrote. "His pallid shadow can never extinguish her light. I carry the scars of Jill's death because that's how I remember to carry her light inside me. The polar contrast between Jill and her killer are so clearly bookends of the extremity of good and evil, and it sometimes feels like an ancient tragedy played out in real life." His words could have easily come out of the mouth of Aaron Leeson-Woolley, who too had been touched by a person who represented everything that was good and then by a person who was pure evil.

Australians were outraged and horrified after learning of Jill's death. Many expressed fear to venture out alone.

Controversial broadcaster Derryn Hinch, who created the Derryn Hinch Justice Party, was so outraged to discover Jill's killer was on bail at the time of the offence that he broke a court order stating the offender could not be named and served 50 days in jail. Mr Hinch said he believed Jill would still be alive if a Geelong magistrate had "done his job." He told *The Geelong Advertiser* that Jill's killer had knocked a man out outside a bar while on parole. "For this he was given a three month sentence. Only three months for knocking a man out—a guy with his criminal record—and then he appealed against the severity of his sentence, three months, and a magistrate gave him bail—and while he was on bail and still on parole, he raped and murdered Jill Meagher. The magistrate should have refused bail and reported to the parole board and said 'hey, this guy's a threat,' and they'd have revoked his parole." Mr Hinch said he did not regret his actions. He would have named the bastard who killed Jill again if he had his time over. "I'm not sorry I did it," he said. "It was the right thing to do."

In 2016, Coroner Ian Gray said Jill Meagher's death was preventable. "A more rigorous, risk-averse approach… would have led to a cancellation of Bayley's parole," he said. "The approach taken is difficult to understand… it did not bring dangerous and high-risk parolees immediately to account."

On the Pedestrian TV website, a writer posted an anonymous article about how Jill's death had shaken her to the core. "It is an acutely sad feeling to know that there are evil people in the world," she wrote. "Today we learned an innocent 29-year-old woman was raped and murdered in what we knew so far to be a random act by a stranger acting on a whim. I think that is the part of the Jill Meagher story that is so incomprehensively fucked up, that this crime may have been a completely unmotivated act by an opportunistic psychopath." They continued by saying that the truth was these things happen.

"And they happen to people like you and me," she wrote. "I got abducted when I was 19." The journalist said she was drunk and decided to walk home. About 1500 metres from her destination, she was pulled into a car. "It took about 30 seconds to realise that I was actually in the backseat of a completely unfamiliar car with two men I had never seen before in my life," she said. "That sobered me up pretty quickly, and when the car started heading toward the bushland on Brisbane's Mount Coot-tha I realised I was probably going to be at least raped, if not hurt or killed."

She said she told the two men she needed to pee. Thinking on her feet, she told them they should stop and allow her to urinate—otherwise her DNA would be all over their car. When the car stopped, she was able to escape after kneeing one of the offenders in the groin. The woman said people should not live their life in fear, but be mindful that there are "some fucked up people in the world who might want to hurt you for some reason."

***

The lack of emotion Vincent Stanford displayed during each of his police interviews was striking. He detailed how he ended the life of the school teacher—all the while appearing calm with his hands resting in his lap. If he felt even a shred of guilt it was not evident, telling police "I went about my day" after Stephanie was dead. It took some prodding, but he eventually told police that he took Stephanie's body to Cocoparra National Park after killing her. One thing that was surprising to police—perhaps because it indicated Vincent may have some sort of remorse for his actions—was that he quickly admitted to killing Stephanie but initially denied raping her. However, he did ultimately decide to plead guilty to both charges.

Vincent told the officers interviewing him that they would find key pieces of evidence at his home in Maiden Avenue. He also told them they would find blood in the room in which she was killed at Leeton High School, despite his best efforts to clean it with a pressure cleaner. He calmly recounted how he drove Stephanie's body—in her vehicle—to Cocoparra National Park in the early hours of Monday morning, after killing her earlier that day. "The time I got there might have been 2am in the morning," Stanford told police.

His memory of the day didn't waver, but when he was asked why he did certain things, he struggled to come up with an answer.

"I think I might have some mental problems," he eventually admitted.

Vincent told police he had dumped Stephanie's car after taking her body to Cocoparra National Park then walked several kilometres home.

Police asked Vincent about the number of scratches on his face. "When did she do that?"

"When I tried to… when I killed her," he replied without emotion.

He told police that when he saw Stephanie working on her computer in the staff room at Leeton High School on Easter Sunday, something came over him.

When asked by police to describe the feeling, he said: "That I had to kill her. I wasn't angry or anything. I was emotionless—just that I had to kill her." Vincent told police that just before he grabbed Stephanie, she said to him: "I'm going, have a happy Easter."

Vincent was extremely candid in his police interviews, but there were some facts the judge ultimately disputed. What Vincent did tell them was, "I went to high school about 7.30, worked for a couple of hours." He had gone to the school to work because he was bored. "Just wanted to go to work." he had said.

Vincent first saw Stephanie when she was in the staff room working on her computer. When she was done, she headed for the school exit. She saw Vincent and, in her usual friendly manner, told him: "I'm going now. Have a good Easter." Just like she had done to each and every person she had encountered in any aspect of her life, she shared a genuine smile and a cheerful greeting. It was just who she was.

Stephanie clearly did not feel any imminent danger before she was attacked from behind while attempting to find her keys in her handbag. How tragic that her trusting nature put her in such a vulnerable position. "When she was ready to leave about 11.30 I took her into the store [room] and killed her," Vincent told police.

When sharing these details, Vincent appeared smug, almost proud of his actions. He told police he put his right arm over Stephanie's mouth and his left arm around her middle. She struggled violently as he walked backwards, dragging her along a corridor to a storeroom which had previously been used as a photography darkroom. Stephanie put up a good fight, scratching Vincent's face and yelling for help, but sadly the sadistic killer was too strong.

He told police he had had a lot of violent thoughts in the past but had never acted on them before. He said he had entertained the idea of hurting or killing various people he had met.

Vincent was asked why he was angry at Stephanie Scott. He replied coldly that he wasn't angry, that he just wanted to kill her. That was a foreign concept for police and the public who would later learn of this detail.

In a second police video, Vincent again sat calmly with his hands on the table. He could have easily been at a bank opening a new account—that was how unaffected he appeared by the whole thing. The fact that he was facing life in prison didn't seem to weigh on him. The fact that he had destroyed the lives of so many didn't seem to keep him up at night. In fact, he actually said he enjoyed the solitude that the walls of a jail cell offered. He showed no reluctance to answer the numerous questions asked about the murder. In fact he showed no emotion at all.

Vincent was asked where he put Stephanie's earrings and engagement ring. He told them he didn't remember. He threw his hands up and said: "I don't know, chucked so much stuff out." Police asked whether he got rid of the ring along with Stephanie's clothes and other belongings. He told police he would have disposed of the ring in a bin somewhere.

"But you do remember taking her engagement ring off her finger at the school?" the police officers asked. "Yeah, she wore two rings," Vincent replied.

Police, confused that Vincent would take the time to remove her rings, asked him what had prompted him to do so.

"I don't know, I was just scrambling up her stuff, making sure I didn't leave anything behind."

Police pressed Vincent on this issue, where the engagement ring was, for some time. "It would be in a bin somewhere, but I have no idea where," he told them.

The reason for this would become clear later on when further details of the day in question were revealed.

At times, Vincent seemed to question his own behaviour. When asked why he kept

Stephanie's bra he callously replied: "I honestly don't know. Maybe I wanted a souvenir."

"Something to remember it by?" the police officer asked him.

"Probably, I had no real reason to keep it."

It is believed taking trophies helps a psychopath prolong the fantasy of the act they committed, although it is unknown whether this is the case with Stanford because he told police he rarely thought about the day he killed Stephanie.

# Chapter Eleven

Aaron Leeson-Woolley was clearly touched by the outpouring of emotion and support. "A massive thankyou to everyone for all their support," he wrote on his Facebook page.

Stephanie's sister Kim wrote on her Facebook page a month after the tragic loss. "1 month today and instead of thinking about how she was taken, we should all try and remember how much Stephanie gave. And what better way to reminisce with your loved ones, over her favourite beverage… a hot cuppa tea."

Stephanie was the fourth born child to Robert and Merrilyn. She had two brothers—Gordon and Stuart, and two sisters—Robyn and Kim. When Kim didn't hear from her sister on her 29th birthday on April 6, she knew something was terribly wrong. "That's how we knew she was missing because I didn't get any messages from her on my birthday," Kim later said. She said her sister would set an alarm to remind herself to wish family and friends a happy birthday after the clock struck 12.01. Kim said it was her father who first called Stephanie "button-nose." "We've all got larger noses and she's got this nice little cute thing," Kim said. Kim also said Stephanie, who was godmother to her other sister Robyn's son, Sam, would have been an amazing mother. Kim said one of her most prized possessions was a ring she wore every day. It was a gift from Stephanie. Kim said Stephanie was always thinking of others. She said when their parents lost their dads in the same year, Stephanie suggested the family play Scattergories on Christmas Day. Kim said she knew her parents were grieving and sad their fathers were absent from the celebration, and this was her way of distracting them and trying to put a smile on their faces. Kim said Stephanie loved gardening and would send her photos of her "little garden" all the time. "Whenever mum came to visit she would take her to the little nursery," she said. She added that the family bought some natives and daffodils and planted them at the site where Stephanie's body was found. "We all went out there together and planted everything for her," Kim said. They felt they owed it to Stephanie to make it a place of beauty, not of pain.

Stephanie's mother Merrilyn described the first time police took the family to the place where a monster had dumped her daughter's body. "We were driven to the desolate place where Stephanie had been left, betrayed, violated and burnt beyond recognition," she said. "It was confronting to see the ground, charred and destroyed where the police had used a metal detector to try and locate her precious rings amongst the ashes."

Stephanie's family members were not the only ones who had lost sleep waiting for answers. Media outlets trying to paint a picture of the man who had brought fear to the residents of Leeton set out to find out anything they could.

It was soon revealed that Vincent Stanford had a violent past. Stanford's nickname among classmates at Prins Florisschool was "Psycho" because of his violent rages. "He was not really all there. He would lose his temper and start throwing things around in the classroom," a classmate later reported. Vincent and his twin were bullied at school. Their slight Australian accents became the butt of many jokes. Despite their size and strength, they didn't fight back—not even verbally. They just walked away. At age 12 Vincent was found on school grounds out of school hours and reprimanded by a teacher. Records show that the teacher grabbed Vincent's coat and he reacted by putting his hands around her neck—making her momentarily fear for her life. Just like dozens of psychopaths before him, he expressed no remorse. That incident led to Vincent being placed at a psychiatric centre where he was diagnosed with autism. When he was released he was sent to a school for children with special needs.

The Stanford family was described as polite by neighbours in the Dutch city of Zoetermeer. On occasion, Vincent would help neighbours with their groceries, but many recalled thinking the family was weird and there was something strange about the young man with the soft voice and seeming inability to look anyone in the eye.

Leeton's Lyn Middleton said she had met Vincent and his mother at her workplace. "She was always quiet, head down, almost in a bit of a shell," she said. Ms Middleton added she didn't notice anything out of the ordinary about Vincent. "There was nothing about him that would make you think that [murder] was coming," she said.

Vincent and his twin Marcus were born in Franklin in Tasmania but their mother moved them to The Netherlands when they were six. Her marriage to their father was over and the boys would never see or hear from him again for many years—a fact that haunted Vincent his entire life. Marcus formed Bullet Proof Studios, a game design company, and Vincent helped with some of the 2D modelling for a number of games, but the company was eventually dissolved.

Vincent worked for a cleaning company and later at a packing and shipping company. His fellow employees and employer were stunned by his brute strength. His former employer Mireille Antonisse told *The Daily Mail* that Vincent had trouble reading social situations and would hardly ever speak. "He is a big guy and exceptionally strong. I think it is part of his condition. If he shut a tap even my husband could not open it again." She added that Stanford's colleagues nicknamed him King Kong because he could lift two crates with one hand like it was nothing. She said Stanford displayed traits of autism such as disliking when his routine changed. "He would get angry if he was cleaning and then halfway through got sent on another job."

Pierre Vandersteen, a friend of Vincent's said Vincent didn't have much of a social life and had trouble forming relationships with women. "He never had a girlfriend in his life because of his autism," he said. "He had a problem connecting to people so he couldn't look a girl in the eye or speak to her. He was more comfortable talking to animals than people."

Mr Vandersteen also said that Vincent was extremely close to his mother, giving her all the money he earnt for groceries and bills. He said the two of them would play darts and backgammon together.

# Chapter Twelve

In early March 2015, Vincent Stanford found a job as a relief cleaner at Leeton High School. It was a temporary position and his employment was supposed to terminate well before Easter Sunday—the day he murdered Stephanie Scott. But in a twist of fate that would prove tragic, his employment at the school was extended.

Vincent's role at the school was limited, and he was not authorised to be on school grounds on weekends. For reasons Vincent has not revealed, he was able to somehow obtain the combination to the alarm system and a set of keys to the school. There was no good reason for him to possess either, though it is perhaps not surprising that he sought both. By having unlimited access to the school grounds, including lockers, classrooms, desks, and other private areas of the school, he could play out any number of sordid fantasies outside of the view of the school staff or even the other cleaners.

Vincent's work was to be completed before and after school hours, 3:30am to 8:30am and 3pm to 6pm. He had no business being at the school when the students or teachers were present. And yet, there were numerous times he was witnessed entering and leaving the girls' toilets during school hours. That alone should have raised several red flags. Yet it wasn't until after Stephanie's murder that the true import of his behaviour would be known.

It was later discovered that around this same time period, Vincent had begun stalking a 12-year-old girl. After his arrest for Stephanie's murder, the police discovered that he had more than 1800 photos of the girl on his computer, along with an exercise book full of details pertaining to her schedule and times when she may be home alone. He had recorded the registration numbers of cars belonging to her family members and noted times when she left the house for ballet and school and when she returned. The exercise book also contained drawings of females, a car, a gun, a sword and an image of a female head with a knife striking it. Stupefying drugs including Valium, Chloroform, Nitrous Oxide and Rohypnol were listed on another page. In what would have been a frightening revelation for Joanne's parents, Stanford also had a laminated photo of a school dance group that she was a part of. He had stolen the photo from a school notice board.

It would later be found that Vincent had written notes specifically about times when he observed the girl was home alone—including the chilling statement: *Home alone 15.40— time enough to abduct.*

He later confessed—in the cold, remorseless tone that would shake Leeton residents to their cores—that he probably would have killed the young girl if he had abducted her. He said it as matter of factly as if he was talking about wanting to buy a Coca Cola at a shop but deciding against it. Through some miracle, he never acted on his impulse to abduct and kill her. Sadly, this was not the case with Stephanie.

It is not known whether Vincent had stalked others in his younger years while living in the Netherlands. It's also not known whether his dark desires heightened as he got older. What is clear is that in the months leading up to that fateful day in April 2015, Vincent spent countless hours obsessing about a number of potential targets—not just the 12-year-old girl.

His second target was a young woman who worked at a Leeton supermarket, referred to as Jillian by the court. On weekly visits to her place of work, Vincent struck up general conversations with her and police discovered he had conducted a number of searches on his computer in an attempt to learn more about her. His lack of social skills meant he was awkward when around her. The woman was friendly and polite, but when she arrived at work early one day to find Vincent sitting in his ute in the carpark, instinct told her to remain in her vehicle until other staff members came. She was relieved when two male co-workers arrived a short time later and she walked alongside them into the supermarket. Her instinct proved correct—police later found photos Vincent had taken of the woman while she was in her car that morning. The fact she decided to trust her intuition and err on the side of caution that morning would later haunt her and make her wonder what if.

A third target of Vincent's was one of Stephanie's colleagues—a 28-year-old teacher at Leeton High School, referred to as Jennifer in court. She often stayed late at school to tidy up and prepare for the next day, a fact Vincent soon became aware of. He began to monitor her movements. Chillingly, the man whose internet history showed he had searched various stupefying drugs would at times be near her car when she left the school for the day. Jennifer later told police she would sometimes say hello and Vincent would say hello back.

Like Stephanie, the teacher was polite, greeting the man who had secretly compiled a dossier of information on her, including at least one photograph of her car parked outside the school.

Vincent had also conducted a number of internet searches in relation to violent rape. These other women still think about how close they came to being Stanford's victim. "There can be no question that the offender is a very disturbed individual," Justice Hulme would later say.

# Chapter Thirteen

By his own admission, Vincent's intentions with the women were not of a romantic nature. He told a psychologist that a girlfriend was "not something [he] craved in life." It is not known why those three escaped with their lives, while a woman he claimed to have never met did not. It's likely he got to a point in time where he felt he could no longer contain his desire to kill. A psychopath who has never felt guilt, empathy or remorse gets to a point where they can no longer see a reason to deny themselves that desire. This is a concept that is almost impossible to understand. Journalist Jon Ronson, author of *The Psychopath Test*, attempted to explain it by lamenting that "psychopathy is probably the most pleasant-feeling of all the mental disorders." Why?

Because the things that keep our behaviour in check, our moral compass, are painful things—guilt, remorse, empathy.

In the book *Mind Behind the Crime*, psychologist and Deakin University Adjunct Professor Helen McGrath said Vincent most likely killed Stephanie because he had a combination of criminal autistic psychopathy and a sexual sadism disorder. Professor Michael Fitzgerald describes a person who has criminal autistic psychopathy as someone who has an autism spectrum disorder as well as antisocial personality disorder, which many see as a mild form of psychopathy. These individuals have an extreme lack of empathy and remorse, limited conscience and are prone to using people cruelly for their own ends. Vincent's sexual sadism disorder meant he had a sexual interest in inflicting humiliation, suffering and pain on another person. "Stanford had secretly fed his obsession over a long period of time, and came close to attacking other young women before he decided to rape and kill Stephanie Scott," Dr McGrath said. "For some reason, on that day, he could no longer resist the urge to act on his sadistic fantasies. It appears that this seemingly quiet young man had several very dark secrets that either did not fully emerge or were not dealt with until it was too late." Dr McGrath added that Vincent lacked empathy for his victim and was obsessed with sexual violence. According to Dr McGrath, he most likely killed the young teacher for the "thrill" he got from sexually assaulting her and then killing her. Dr McGrath suggested the combination of traits Vincent had was rare and not easy to identify. "Few people saw him as potentially violent, and his neighbours found him to be personable if a little strange." The traits Vincent possessed were a "horrifying combination," Dr McGrath shared. "His callous, cold-blooded and sadistic actions would have caused Stephanie Scott great fear, pain and suffering," she said.

The sad reality is that it is almost impossible to try to make sense of any part of the crime that would shake countless people to the core and make them question how one man could break the heart of a nation and later say he rarely thought about the day he took Stephanie's life. The heartbreak people felt soon turned to anger for many and made them question their faith in humanity.

But even in death, Stephanie helped people see the light.

Her family made sure of that.

And for that they should be eternally proud.

# Chapter Fourteen

When Vincent Stanford and his family arrived in Leeton with few possessions, neighbours spoke about the odd sight of Vincent seemingly having nothing but a mattress and a bag. The lack of belongings was enough to spur the rumour mill into action, but those hungry for a slice of juicy gossip were left wanting. The family, while quiet, didn't appear to have any obvious skeletons in their closet. They all worked, kept to themselves and didn't give their neighbours any grief. The initial interest in them waned and life went back to normal. The modest rental home they moved into was soon full of the inviting aroma of freshly baked scones generously dropped off by residents keen to welcome the new additions to their town, and the Stanford family's kitchen drawers soon contained borrowed utensils.

By all accounts Vincent was soft spoken and polite.

After Stephanie's murder, a number of residents spoke to journalists in their typically friendly manner, sharing what they knew, only to regret it later when their words were twisted to suit the story of the day. A pushy journalist asked one couple, who were only referred to as Bill and Gail, about their neighbours—the Stanfords. They described Vincent as "lovely." "I found him a very nice, well-mannered young fellow," Gail said. When later contacted by another journalist, they were steadfast in their resolve that they no longer wanted to speak the media. It was clear that they had been told their words had added in some way to the hurt the town was feeling—and that was the last thing they had wanted to do. They had felt pushed into a corner by the hardened reporter who knew what he wanted them to say.

Meanwhile, Vincent had been convinced that a move back to Australia, the country where he was born, would be his ticket to gaming success. For the first time in a very long time, he was hopeful. It was rare for him to experience such feelings. He was usually detached from the world, often described as someone who was void of emotions. He was content when he was alone, finding the company of others stressful, and had no friends to speak of. Gaming was one of the few things in life that brought him a sense of happiness.

Vincent had a number of goals in life, which he worked hard to achieve. However, rejection would become a constant for him, leading to resentment. His bids to study information technology and to join the Army were unsuccessful. The latter was something that hit him hard. Then his attempts to break into the gaming industry proved fruitless, as did his efforts to gain employment for months on end. He reluctantly picked up work as a cleaner in the Netherlands, a role that suited him due to its lack of a requirement for social interaction. But it wasn't the fresh start he had dreamed about and, over time, his resentment and anger would grow.

Like he was in other aspects of his life, he became meticulous about his cleaner role.

However, his boss' lack of attention to detail fuelled Vincent's anger. Vincent thought his boss had a "close enough is good enough" attitude and this lax approach made him see red.

Vincent later said he had serious thoughts of violence against his boss, expressing frustration that the man was disorganised and did not care about the standards of his workers. As time went by, the continued examples of this became a thorn in Vincent's side. He fantasized about hurting his boss and, like he did in all aspects of his life, justified these thoughts by telling himself it was the actions of his boss that were to blame, not his own unnatural desire to hurt others. A psychopath often sees himself as a hero or victim, never the villain.

Eventually, Vincent recognised the best outcome for everyone would be to remove himself from the potentially lethal situation. For Vincent, it was "time to leave."

Sadly, there would come a moment when this logical thinking and restraint was not exercised and the consequences would be catastrophic. Like many psychopaths, there would eventually come a time when his evil ways would lead to tragedy.

# Chapter Fifteen

Stephanie Scott was a dedicated school teacher both inside the classroom and out of it. She was preparing for her wedding and honeymoon, but before she could turn her full attention to these impending events, she wanted to ensure she had ticked all the I's and crossed all the T's when it came to the plan for her students in her absence. She wanted to arrive in Tahiti with her new husband buoyed by the knowledge that the transition for the relief teacher would be a smooth one.

On the last day of school before the Easter holidays and a week before her wedding, students and fellow teachers wished Stephanie well. Her colleagues threw a party for her on that day. The radiance that exuded from Stephanie when she spoke about her wedding was something no one would ever forget.

Good Friday fell on the next day, and Aaron was heading home to Canowindra for a party that was being held for a mutual friend of the couple. Stephanie had decided to stay home and complete the plan for the relief teacher and finish off some shopping in Griffith before the wedding.

When Aaron left for Canowindra, he told his fiancée he loved her and the couple remained in touch throughout the weekend via calls and SMS messages (texts). Aaron would later say the couple never went more than a few hours without checking in on each other.

Stephanie spoke to her sister Robyn on Saturday night and told her the final touches for her wedding in Eugowra, which would be attended by more than 100 guests, were coming together. Family and friends were coming from all over for the affair, including from overseas. Robyn said that when she spoke to her Stephanie was riding on a cloud of anticipation. She could barely contain her excitement at marrying the man of her dreams and celebrating with family and friends.

Stephanie told her older sister that she had been to Griffith shopping and had picked up some cufflinks for her husband-to-be and his groomsmen and a bikini for the couple's honeymoon.

Easter Sunday, April 5, 2015, was a mild day in Leeton. The sun was shining—a sure sign to Stephanie that everything would be perfect, including the weather, on her wedding day the following week.

Stephanie decided to head into school one final time before beginning her holiday. Unlike Vincent Stanford, she did not have a key or alarm access codes. Instead, she dropped into the home of a colleague, Monique Hardy, who accompanied her to the school to help her get in.

Neither of the women were expecting anyone else to be there.

Shortly before 1pm, after several hours spent at the school, Stephanie sent an email to confirm a wedding expense. She deactivated the alarm for the school's administration block at 1.31 pm and re-armed it seven minutes later. She then headed to her car, content that she had made things as easy as possible for the relief teacher while she would be enjoying her first days of married life.

"I'm going home now," she told Vincent Stanford when she encountered him on her way to the carpark. "Have a happy Easter."

Sadly, Vincent had much more sinister plans.

# Chapter Sixteen

In the days after Vincent Stanford was arrested, there was speculation he may not have acted alone. How did he get home from where he dumped Stephanie's car in a paddock about 10 kilometres outside of Leeton? This was a question that many asked.

On June 10, 2015, two months after Stephanie's murder, police arrested Vincent's identical twin Marcus. This development sent shockwaves through the community of Leeton and into households across Australia. Police revealed they would seek to have Marcus extradited from South Australia to NSW, where he would be charged with being an accessory after the fact in relation to Stephanie's murder. If found guilty, Marcus could face a sentence of up to 25 years in prison for his role in the crime. This revelation came just a week after Vincent was hit with a further charge of aggravated sexual assault against Stephanie.

The public was desperate to know what the twin's involvement may have been, and soon discovered it potentially included helping Vincent dispose of the body, to hide or get rid of incriminating evidence, or to help a person flee the scene of the crime. It could also relate to deliberately lying to cover up the crime or the identity of the principal offender.

When Vincent was arrested, they had deemed it necessary to interview Marcus to ensure they "had the right person in custody, given they had learned from Vincent Stanford's mother that he had a twin brother." There have been cases around the world where identical twins have been able to get away with committing a crime by blaming it on their sibling who shares the same DNA.

Marcus was first interviewed by South Australian police at the Mount Barker police station on Tuesday, April 21. He told police he spoke to his brother on Saturday, April 4, the day before the murder. He said his brother seemed normal. However, the following day Vincent called Marcus about 6.56pm and Marcus deemed his twin's behaviour to be "weird."

When Marcus asked what he was doing Vincent said: "Just driving around." When he pressed him about where he was going, he again replied: "Just driving around."

On Wednesday, April 8 Marcus again spoke to his brother. On this occasion, Marcus told police, his brother appeared to be back to his usual self.

Marcus told police he saw a television news report the next day about a murder in Leeton. The report revealed a 24-year-old cleaner at a school had been arrested. Marcus shared he felt sick and immediately called his mother, who confirmed it was Vincent who had been arrested.

What Marcus omitted to tell police was that he had exchanged a series of text messages with his brother the day before. "I'm going to send you an envelope, keep it safe for me," Vincent wrote to his brother. "Can you let me know when you receive the envelope?" he added.

Inside the envelope were Stephanie's engagement and graduation rings—two of her most prized possessions.

The news that Marcus had not only received but sold Stephanie's engagement ring to help his brother was a further blow to the Scott family. Police discovered that on Tuesday, April 14 Marcus conducted an internet search for "selling jewellery in Adelaide."

On Monday, May 4 he conducted further searches on the value of diamond engagement rings.

On May 9 he took the two rings Stephanie had been wearing at the time of her death to the Adelaide Exchange Jewellery store in Modbury in South Australia. Marcus was paid $705 for the two rings, which could now never be returned to the family because they had been "scrapped."

On May 26, Vincent called Marcus from prison. When asked what he did with the stuff he was sent in the envelope, Marcus replied: "Exactly what you told me to do."

"Did you get a bit for it or…?" Vincent asked.

"Yeah, yeah, yeah," was the reply.

When asked by police on May 30, Marcus denied being sent the jewellery in the mail.

However, on August 5, Marcus confessed to police that he had received the two rings along with Stephanie's driver's licence in the mail. He told police he used some of the money he received for the rings to allow him to visit Vincent in prison in Sydney.

Marcus also told police he took two photos of the licence and then burnt it. "At the time I thought in case I ever needed to show police, but I'm not too sure exactly why."

When asked why he helped his brother, he told police it was "misplaced loyalty."

# Chapter Seventeen

Six months after Stephanie's death her family was forced to mark her 27th birthday without her. Instead of celebrating the fact that she was not only a year older but also a Mrs, the family once again choked back tears on October 14 and asked members of the public to have a cup of tea at 3pm—the time Stephanie was born. "Have a cuppa for our Stephanie. Forever 26," Kim wrote on her Facebook page. "Who knew on this day 27 years ago an angel like you would be born," she said. "Although you weren't a boy as dad first thought, we wouldn't have had you any other way. To say we were lucky is an understatement. To the girl who defines the word 'fun-loving,' happy birthday. I'm so proud to call you my little sister. And although you may not be here, I'm sure you'll be sprinkling a few hundreds and thousands in heaven today."

The wheels of justice turn quite slowly. The family's wait to have their chance to share the horror of what they had been through in court wouldn't come for over another year. But when it did, they again amazed all with their enduring strength.

Stephanie's mother Merrilyn Scott bravely read a victim impact statement in court, revealing how devastated she and other family members were. She was as strong as ever. She did her daughter proud. Her steely gaze was that of a mother scorned, a look of determination that said *you've taken so much from us, you heartless bastard, you're not taking this moment*. On this occasion they were in court to deal with the involvement Marcus had in the murder. "As with everything we have had to face in the past 16 months, we do this for the love of our precious Stephanie," she said. She added that the family was shattered by the senseless tragedy.

Merrilyn put it so astutely when she said she had not worried about Stephanie's safety when she moved to Leeton. "We thought she would be safe," she said.

The hearing was a bittersweet moment—one that she and her family had waited for, a chance to speak on behalf of their daughter. The bond the Scott family had with Aaron was clear for all to see. He was always flanked by Stephanie's family members, who appeared to instinctively try to shield him from the prying eyes, the invasive microphones.

"I write on behalf of our shattered family and of Aaron, who is and probably always will be too deeply affected to put into words the depth of his grief and sorrow," Mrs Scott said.

Mrs Scott also said Stephanie was the communicator in the family. "We had an amazing girl and she is gone. Losing Stephanie is a tragedy that has impacted us all very deeply. We are destined to live a life unfulfilled—how can we be fulfilled when part of us is missing?"

Mrs Scott explained that it was hard to forgive Marcus for his role, no matter how small, in taking another thing away from the family. She said the family had been devastated to learn that Stephanie's rings were gone forever. "When Stephanie completed her degree we bought her a ring of her choosing, as we had done with her sisters," Mrs Scott said. "Her engagement ring was of Aaron's choosing, presented to Stephanie as a symbol of their love and commitment to each other." The engagement ring held the promise of a lifetime together. "Two little rings. How significant they were in life, and now in death," Mrs Scott said.

She said the family could not comprehend the actions of Vincent and his twin brother Marcus. "Even as we searched, Stephanie's fate was known by a second person. Both were part of something so monstrous, so cruel and heartless, devoid of any of the qualities that make us moral human beings. Opportunities to assist the police were squandered, and now we must all suffer the consequences."

Mrs Scott praised the police for going to great lengths to recover the rings. "They could see that having them returned to us would be a great help, when so much had been taken away."

Mrs Scott said it was devastating to discover the rings that had meant so much to Stephanie had become trophies. She said the vision of them being removed from Stephanie's gentle, loving hands made her feel sick to her stomach and filled her with despair. She choked back tears as she told the court they could never be returned. She said the family was shocked to learn the rings had been sold to the lowest bidder, an act she described as "mercenary, full of greed and so damning. Even more callous and contemptible, the proceeds were used for a flight to visit [Vincent in] Silverwater prison."

In a further blow, the family also learnt that Stephanie's driver's licence had been sent as a trophy to Vincent's twin, Marcus. "It was removed from her purse, an act I find infuriating and disgusting," Mrs Scott said. It was distressing to learn Marcus had photographed the licence after it arrived in the mail. "Even after seeing this most important and personal photograph of our daughter, there was no sign of conscience, no thought to assist the police." She said the bond shared between the twins was sinister, frightening and dangerous. She told the court that they conspired to conceal the truth but were ultimately caught due to their own greed and arrogance.

Mrs Scott said her daughter represented all that was good about humankind. "She possessed all the qualities we value and was a source of pride, joy and inspiration to our family, her many friends and all who knew her." Mrs Scott said the loss of Stephanie had turned her family upside down. "What a tragedy! What a waste! It has affected every hour of every day." She told the court there had been many wakeless nights which were haunted by visions no family should have to know. "A day has not passed that we have not shed a tear for our beautiful girl and for all that has been taken from her."

Mrs Scott said it was still hard to imagine a future without Stephanie in it. And when people stopped in her the street to pass on their condolences and ask about her daughter, she found it hard to put into words just how special Stephanie had been. She said the family members experienced myriad emotions each and every day—sometimes the full spectrum in a single hour. They had all found it difficult to return to work. "We are all angry. We have no tolerance for triviality. There is no peace."

Mrs Scott said grief was exhausting and darkness followed each family member like a cloud. She said she no longer got joy from listening to music. Like many people touched by tragedy, she found her thoughts turning to Stephanie and what she had experienced, making moments of happiness fleeting and rare. "I am tearful, have difficulty concentrating and am constantly distracted."

Mrs Scott shared that she had missed appointments, suffered ill health and lost weight, a fact no one could deny. Her face appeared gaunt, her eyes haunted. "I no longer enjoy pastimes, I find going to the shop alone too hard and I have little interest in the future. These are supposed to be the golden years, but for us they are not…."

Mrs Scott said she was proud of the way her family had been dealing with the crippling pain. "Through all these difficult and heartbreaking months our children have handled themselves with courage and grace."

Mrs Scott said grieving in the public eye has been difficult. "I also acknowledge and thank my husband for his courage, his strength, and his love and patience. As our second year of birthdays, anniversaries and special family occasions without Stephanie passes, we steel ourselves for the months and years ahead. There will be no end to the sorrow we feel and we can never make sense of losing our beautiful girl. She had only good in her heart and was so loved by us all."

Dr Katie Seidler, a clinical and forensic psychologist, prepared a report on Marcus Stanford that was presented at his trial. She said Marcus described himself as a somewhat shy and disengaged individual socially. He put this down to anxiety. Marcus admitted he began abusing both alcohol and cannabis when he was a teenager. Dr Seidler said she believed this led to him being irresponsible and unproductive at times.

Marcus' solicitor Bill Neild concluded that Marcus was a person of otherwise good character, based on his previously clean criminal record and history of gainful employment. He said his client was genuinely remorseful, but Justice Robert Hulme said he did not accept that. He said Dr Seidler's report also indicated Marcus Stanford expressed both remorse and regret, but there was insufficient evidence to support that. However, Justice Hulme said: "I am prepared to accept the submission that the offender is unlikely to reoffend and has good prospects of rehabilitation. This is primarily on the basis that the present offence was committed in a highly specific and unusual context and the offender has not otherwise demonstrated any tendency to criminal offending."

# Chapter Eighteen

There was widespread outrage after Marcus' sentence of 15 months was handed down. Many believed it was too lenient. Stephanie's family was devastated when they heard the news.

Superintendent Michael Rowan said that the family was "shattered." He said he didn't know if any punishment could ease their pain but said the family had expected more. However, he conceded the sentence was what police were expecting, based on sentencing guidelines. Despite this he said he did not believe the community would agree with the sentence.

Leeton mayor Paul Maytom urged the community to accept the sentence the court had imposed, but admitted it left an extremely bitter taste in everyone's mouths. He said his thoughts were with Stephanie's family and friends.

Marcus later apologised to Stephanie's family for doing a "really stupid thing." He said he was sorry for the hurt he had caused them. But the words seemed hollow coming from the mouth of a man who appeared to be sharing a joke with a prison officer on the video link up to the court during his sentencing hearing.

Mark Norvall, a Leeton resident and father of one of Stephanie's students, was infuriated by the sentence. He launched an online petition asking the Director of Public Prosecutions to appeal against the sentence on the grounds it was too lenient.

"This is a petition to the NSW Department of Public Prosecutions to appeal the pathetic 15-month sentence handed down to Marcus Stanford for being an accessory after the fact of Stephanie Scott's murder by his brother Vincent," he wrote in a Facebook post.

The post was shared dozens of times and signed by more than 70,000 people. Mr Norvall said he had helped search for

Stephanie in the days after her disappearance, convinced she would be found safe and well. Mr Norvall was incensed that Marcus, who had been remanded in custody after his arrest, would now be free to do as he pleased in 15 days based on time served. It made him feel sick to his stomach, he said. "The injustice is shocking. I cannot imagine how Stephanie's family are feeling knowing that someone who played such a key role in their daughter's death is getting off so lightly."

Mr Norvall said the sentence was "pathetic." He said Marcus' apology was "too little, too late." "It's just not good enough," he said. "If you watch the video clip he [Marcus] says it all with a smug grin on his face, like [he is saying] I got away with it."

Mr Norvall added that the lenient sentence was a horrendous blow to a nation that was nursing a broken heart. "He even took her wedding rings and jewellery to a pawn shop to cash in on her death."

The fact that a man had sat on the sidelines and watched the whole debacle unravel while armed with information that could have in some small way spared the Scott family some amount of pain hit the public hard. As is often the case with twins, many had speculated that Vincent was the evil twin. But now they wondered if they were both rotten.

"The feeling in the community is one of absolute disbelief, anger and horror at what we feel is a lack of justice and slap-on-the-wrist sentences that are handed down one after another," Mr Norvall told *The Irrigator*. He said he believed a sentence of 10 years would have been more appropriate. "He showed no remorse, he did his utmost to hide that evidence and he sold the rings so he could visit his murderous brother."

Community members took part in a protest march, echoing similar sentiments.

Samantha Buffet, who helped organise the march, said Marcus Stanford should have been given the maximum sentence for his offence—25 years. She said he had treated the rings as if they were nothing. "The family should have been able to get those back, it would help in the grieving process. They won't have that piece of her back ever again.

It's all just such a mess, so heart-breaking and absolutely horrible."

NSW premier Mike Baird directed the Attorney General to look into Marcus' backdated sentence. "Where there is a crime such as this we need the appropriate justice, and certainly on what has been presented that doesn't seem to be the case to me, but again the Attorney General is exploring every possible avenue," Mr Baird said.

The Director or Public Prosecutions (DPP) eventually revealed, "I have decided not to appeal the sentence imposed by Justice Hulme in relation to the charge of accessory after the fact to murder against [Marcus] Stanford. I have formed the view that there are no reasonable prospects of success on an appeal against the inadequacy of the sentence."

And while this came as another slap in the face to the Scott family and the broader public, the judge had done his job—he had acted within the confines of the law. If anything, he was being used as a scapegoat. A more productive action perhaps would have been to push for longer mandatory sentences. But it's easier to have a person to blame—even if deep down you know it's not warranted—than to concede that it was a failing of a system that is almost impossible to take on. Perhaps that's a symptom of our social media loving world. We feel empowered to express our views in an online platform or take to the streets. It feels like a win—even if it isn't. And that's not to say that the actions of the protesters were not appreciated by the Scott family and Aaron, but in the end they proved futile.

One of the people who signed the petition to reconsider the sentence said Stephanie had been her Drama and English teacher. "Once I found out she was missing, I tried everything I could to help find her." This student said she was in denial when the shocking details of the grisly crime were revealed. She added that the tragedy affected every aspect of her life for a full year and the confidence her teacher had instilled in her waned. She said she experienced paranoia and hadn't performed since.

Another wrote: "This is not justice. I do not agree." A number of people expressed their disgust at the sentence on Facebook.

"Stephanie's family and friends deserve better than this," shared a third person. "If this was America it would have been 55 years!"

Barrister Anthony Marinac said he was asked by a friend who lived near Leeton to provide an "explainer" on the Stanford's sentence and the decision by the DPP to not appeal the sentence. "There has been considerable community outrage at the sentencing decision, and concern since the DPP in NSW decided not to pursue an appeal," he wrote on his Facebook page. "Mr Stanford was the identical twin brother of the killer. He was not involved in the murder in any way, and did not in fact know that his brother had committed the murder until his brother was arrested."

Mr Marinac said he knew he was taking a bit of a risk by posting the "explainer." "By explaining the sentencing decision, it might appear that I am somehow supportive of Stanford or his conduct," he said. "Please let me make it as clear as I possibly can that what he did was reprehensible. The outrage being expressed by the Riverina is decent, honest outrage by people who ought to be outraged." Mr Marinac said sentencing was tricky. "When a law provides a sentence, it is the maximum sentence which the judge can apply. In this case the maximum sentence is 25 years in prison. That maximum sentence is meant to be reserved for the worst type of case for each offence. So the court begins by considering whether the current offending is in the worst category."

Mr Marinac went on to explain that the worst types were cases where the offender actually assisted the murderer to dispose of the body of the victim. "Next there is the type of offending which involves helping a murderer to flee justice, either by helping them get away or hiding them from police or something similar." Mr Marinac said there was no suggestion Marcus had done anything like that. He said Marcus' brother was already in custody by the time Marcus realised he was the offender.

Mr Marinac continued by saying that the next type of offending involves disposing of evidence in order to defeat the investigation.

"This is where Stanford starts to run into trouble," he said. "When he received the envelope from his brother, what he really should have done is taken it to the nearest police station, unopened. By selling the rings and burning the licence, he destroyed or disposed of evidence which pretty clearly linked his brother to the victim."

However, Mr Marinac said there was a distinct difference between Marcus' conduct and destroying really crucial evidence, such as bloodstained clothes. "So the bottom line here is that when you can consider all the possible ways that one might assist a murderer, this was pretty low on the scale. It did not cover [up] the crime, did not keep the murderer from justice, and the evidence destroyed was of low evidential value… It was, however, of incredibly important emotional value to the Scott family—and the community clearly shares their outrage." He said the judge also had to consider other mitigating and aggravating factors—factors which suggest a need for greater or lesser punishment. "In this case there were a number of mitigating factors [which decrease the need for punishment]."

He said the law accepted that sometimes accessories act out of a misguided loyalty towards family members. "By acting to support his twin brother, Stanford was acting in a way which is in some small sense understandable."

"Certainly it would be less understandable for him to act in such a way for a perfect stranger, and even less understandable if he had helped cover up the crime for, say, personal gain. So the judge had to take that family motivation into account."

Mr Marinac said the law also accepted that if a person assists the police after their arrest, they have assisted justice and the families of the victim to find closure and should be entitled to a lesser sentence than a person who completely refuses to help police. "If the law didn't accept this, then no criminal would ever comply with police and, frankly, many more criminals would get away with their offences," Mr Marinac said. "In this case, after his arrest, Mr Stanford [eventually] fully confessed his involvement to police and assisted them as much as he could, which would have assisted their investigations in relation to his brother."

Mr Marinac said the final factor was that when a person pleads guilty they are entitled to a sentence discount because they have spared the costs of an investigation and trial and have saved the family of the victim the trauma of enduring a trial. "It seems reasonable that they should receive a lesser sentence than someone who proclaims their innocence despite knowing they are guilty," Mr Marinac said. "Adding all of these factors up, the judge indicated a 'head sentence' of one year and eight months, and then reduced that by a quarter for the early plea of guilty."

Mr Marinac said he believed the DPP decided not to appeal the sentence because the judge's sentence was appropriate. "There is no prospect of an appeal succeeding, and they know it." Mr Marinac said Stephanie's death was a terrible, terrible tragedy. "I cannot even begin to imagine what the Scott family has endured these past 18 months. I completely understand the community's thirst for revenge. In this case, I do believe the sentence was just and appropriate. I wonder if he [Marcus] will ever be able to live with himself though."

People who read Mr Marinac's explanation knew he spoke the truth but they struggled to accept it. The Scott family had been dealt blow after blow. Where was the justice in that?

Kelsey Sutor, a journalist for Fairfax Media, said news of Marcus' release had been met with outrage by a number of her colleagues. "Normally news doesn't get a one-sided reaction in a newsroom, but this announcement was met with anger and disgust. Stanford's sentence was backdated after already serving 15 months in prison, which in my opinion still wasn't long enough." She said it was not the first time justice hadn't been served for a woman who was murdered. "On May 1, 2012, the body of Allison Baden-Clay was found in a creek outside of Brisbane," Ms Sutor said. "Her husband, Gerard Baden-Clay was found guilty of her murder before that charge was downgraded to manslaughter. The community was outraged and, thankfully and even amazingly, that outrage led to the Director of Public Prosecutions attempting to appeal the downgrade, but there is still a possibility of Baden-Clay walking the streets as a free man. How many more women have to die at the hands of violent men? How many more of these violent men will be slapped on the wrist? What sort of message does that send to violent men?"

Ms Suter said Australia had long had a problem with violence against women. "Marcus Stanford isn't a murderer but to allow him to walk free after such a short jail stint sends a seriously scary message—that justice will not prevail for men who stand by and allow this to happen to women." Many people found themselves considering what they would do if a sibling asked for their help after committing an atrocious crime. Most found themselves saying they would do the right thing, they would convince their sibling to turn themselves in. But there was a small part of them that wondered if that would really be the case if they were faced with that reality.

Despite the public outrage, Marcus was released from jail. He returned to South Australia to live in a caravan park on the Yorke Peninsula with his father Steve. When Marcus was released, his father briefly spoke to the media. "I don't understand why Vincent did what he did."

Nothing has been heard of Marcus in the years since Stephanie's death. But there's little doubt that many members of the public will always have a high level of disdain when they hear his name.

# Chapter Nineteen

Vincent Stanford spoke with forensic psychologist Anna Robilliard in the lead up to his trial. He told her he enjoyed sitting in his prison cell, carving scars on his arms and humming the theme song to the television show *MacGyver.* The fact he did not have to talk to people was a great comfort to him, he informed her. He told her he had "alright" relationships with his family members, but admitted he was not very close to his older brother Luke. Ms Robilliard did not find any evidence of drug or alcohol abuse. Vincent told the psychologist that he had a girlfriend at age 14, but had no desire to begin any new relationships when that ended after six months.

A picture of the cold-blooded killer began to emerge when he confessed that when he saw Stephanie Scott on Easter Sunday, 2015, he was immediately overwhelmed with a desire to kill her. "Mr Stanford said he had absolutely no prior plan to murder the victim Stephanie Scott and he did not know her at all," Ms Robilliard said in her report. "As soon as he saw her at the school where he was working, on the morning he murdered her, Mr Stanford said 'I had to kill her.' He said it was an instant thought and that it was not unusual for him to have such thoughts."

Vincent told Ms Robilliard he had had thoughts of killing someone since the age of 7 or 8. "He stated that he gets violent thoughts when people cause him stress," she wrote. "He said it can build up to an almost intolerable level. He said his violent thoughts are usually caused when people interrupt his routine, and in the past this had been triggered by teachers, other students, mental health care nurses and even his mother."

Vincent said these violent thoughts were not usually accompanied by feelings of anger, describing it instead as "just cold-blooded violence." He said he had not been angry with

Stephanie Scott. "He said he had never been bothered by violence: his own or anyone else's. As a child he used to think it was normal and kept it bottled up."

Vincent also told her he now knew his thoughts were not normal, but confessed he still entertained the same violent thoughts. He told her that he had these thoughts usually at least once a week, especially when he had to interact with people because he preferred to be alone. This admission sent chills through the minds of Leeton residents. If he had not been caught, their town may have become even more infamous for being home to a serial killer. Many lost sleep at night as they wrestled with this idea. Stanford said he didn't think there was any way he could change. "This is just the way I'm arranged—I don't think there is anything I can do to get them [the violent thoughts] away," he told Ms Robilliard.

Vincent made it very clear he felt no remorse about the murder. He told the psychologist that, in fact, he hardly ever thought about it. "I can hardly remember it… it was so long ago." Vincent also said he didn't

feel guilty. "This was something I had to do…
I couldn't stop myself."

The school cleaner told her he didn't
enjoy killing Stephanie, but conceded the
act reduced his tension. "He said he did not
entertain the urge to kill anyone for a couple
of months after that and then the same
thoughts returned," Ms Robilliard wrote. "He
also stated that he does not anticipate gaining
pleasure from harming others, just relief from
his own urge to kill."

Vincent said to Ms Robilliard that he
was aware he was different. "I think I've done
remarkably well to live with people for 25
years," he told her. Vincent added that he
didn't think he could change. "I don't think
there are any treatments for my inability to
deal with other people."

Ms Robilliard conducted a number of
psychometric tests on Vincent, one of which
indicated he had "deeply entrenched structural
faults in the personality construct." She said
Vincent struggled to experience emotion
and was extremely detached from society
and indifferent to others. He had an elevated

score on the "sadistic/aggressive" scale, which identifies people likely predisposed toward aggressive outbursts which might be expressed in a callous manner.

However, Vincent only returned a low range score on a test of psychopathy traits. "In most of the facets his scores were in the low or very low range but on the facet which measured lack of remorse, empathy, and unacceptance of responsibility, his score was in the high range," Ms Robilliard wrote. She also noted that Vincent displayed signs of depression. Ms Robilliard did not believe he met the criteria for a diagnosis of Autism Spectrum Disorder. She indicated Vincent's mental state played a part in the murder. "Mr Stanford has developed an entrenched self-belief that he is defective," she wrote. He said she believed Vincent battled with feelings of despair for himself and his unfulfilled expectations, which led to anger and hatred towards others. "He is essentially looking into this internally conflicted state leading to ongoing tension which he described as [having] reached an intolerable level at times."

Ms Robilliard said Vincent believed his strategy for dealing with the tension was to harm himself or others. "He described having one feeling, hatred, which could be a consequence of his perception of exclusion and rejection and the source of a generalised social animosity that may have triggered his angry, unpremeditated and overwhelming urge to kill the victim," she wrote.

Forensic psychologist Professor David Greenberg also provided a report on Vincent. However, in a further act of defiance, another trait of a psychopath who carves his own path in life, not caring about others or the lay of the land, Vincent did not consent to being interviewed by him, which meant Professor Greenberg had to draw his conclusions based on the evidence provided to him. Unlike Ms Robilliard, he said he believed it was highly likely Stanford had Autistic Spectrum Disorder and some features of a psychopathic personality.

Professor Greenburg said he believed Vincent had a likely paraphilic disorder—recurrent, intense, sexually arousing fantasies or behaviours—which played a part in his motivation to murder Stephanie. He pondered whether Vincent had a sexual interest in cross-dressing or fetishism, as a sexy female costume was found in his wardrobe, or bestiality, given he had conducted internet searches relating to sexual acts with dogs and horses.

Professor Greenberg concluded that the risk of Vincent committing further sexual and/or violent acts should be regarded in the "high risk" range. "Relative to the general male population, his risk of sexual violence must be regarded as the highest category," Professor Greenberg wrote. "However, his response to treatment and management may or may not change this risk assessment in the future. At this point, his prognosis should be regarded as guarded."

The media reported that Vincent was an avid online gamer. In fact, one of the sites he was a member of even admitted to the link when Stanford was charged. Documenting Reality posted a message for its members which read: "Just wanted to let everyone know that a member of this site has been accused of murder in Australia last week. Vincent went by the name quetzalcoalt here and was not very active. Think he has like seven posts. The story is tragic, and a beautiful girl named Stephanie Scott allegedly lost her life because of him. Truly a sad situation."

The post also said that media had reported he was "really into Nazi stuff and anything relating to the Waffen-SS." It stated a number of news outlets seemed to be trying to imply there was a link between his love of violent games and the crime he'd committed.

Lauren Rosewarne, a senior lecturer at the University of Melbourne, spoke about this new phenomenon of crimes being linked to violent online gaming. "Chucky and porn were the reasons given for crimes in decades past; now the internet is the bogeyman," she said in an article for ABC news. She said reports of the horrible murder of Stephanie Scott had taken a familiar turn. "Now that the fetishisation of her soon-to-be-bride status has waned, attention has moved to the alleged perp, Vincent Stanford," Ms Rosewarne said. She said news reports were quick to reveal that

Vincent liked violent videos. "Many seemingly unfathomable crimes, in fact, get reported the same way," Ms Rosewarne shared. "Clues are presented to help readers piece together an—albeit hokey—story of how such an atrocity could transpire. By thinking a pattern exists, shaken onlookers can delude themselves into believing that they now know what a warning sign looks like. That such diabolical acts can surely be prevented next time."

Ms Rosewarne explained that these clues took a very specific form in these reports. "Back in 1996 for example, we didn't get information about Martin Byrant's favourite foods or his preferred hair styling products," she said. "Instead, we were informed that he had a fervent interest in Chucky videos, because loving a fictional homicidal doll renders a person deviant within an us vs them culture salivating for easy answers."

Ms Rosewarne added that when Ted Bundy claimed that pornography made him rape and slay more than thirty women, his claim was seized upon as a truth. "Bundy was simply 'confirming' suspicions already rampant in a culture that wants to control pleasure, control media, and is desperately seeking simplistic explanations and 'solutions.'"

Ms Rosewarne said that knowing Vincent likes Nazi marching music and military-themed computer games provided the perfect *aha* moment for an audience that wanted to see murderers as stereotypes, who wanted to believe that media has miraculously transformative powers, who wanted to believe that horrible things can be prevented.

Ms Rosewarne also said that in the internet age the bogeyman of online gaming, of online role play, of cyberspace as a kind of Badlands provides the new magic bullet. "We now know, for example, all about Stanford's online identity as Quetzalcoatl, a mythical Aztec serpent," she said. "We know this because such a slithery, scary avatar can only help to pad out the picture of a cyber creep."

Ms Rosewarne added that the news media loved to allege the internet could somehow create villains. "… In an online world where identity can be played with and reality reinvented, that surely some of this is going to seep into real life."

Ms Rosewarne said excessive internet use was mainstream and far too common to serve as any kind of useful clue. "Pretending therefore that those who game online or play with identity online are somehow different is cruel is indicative of a journalistic laziness and hints at the consumption of one too many episodes of *Criminal Minds*," she said. "Demonisation and stereotypes might embellish a story, but surely a more nuanced approach to understanding the criminal mind is well overdue."

Good points, those who read this might concede. But if he was not a monster of the worst kind, one that only comes along once in a blue moon, then the chances that another Vincent Stanford was living in their neighbourhood, their town, their city, in their daughter's university dorm, were heightened. And that was a possibility people didn't want to even consider.

# Chapter Twenty

In March 2016, the Scott family and Aaron Leeson-Woolley filed into the Griffith Local Court. They walked with a purpose and looked straight ahead, ignoring the people gathered to get a glimpse of them. Stephanie's mother Merrilyn wore a yellow flower pinned to her blue dress. Vincent Stanford appeared via video link from the Metropolitan Remand and Reception Centre. He had his head bowed during the duration of the hearing. Others gathered in the court had looks of disgust on their face as they focused squarely on Vincent on the screen. There was a moment when they thought the monster they were looking at was going to hurt this grieving family once again, when Vincent's solicitor David Davidge requested an adjournment to allow his client to be assessed to find out whether he was fit to stand trial. This request was denied and those in the courtroom breathed a collective sigh of relief. *Enough,* they all seemed to silently say. *Give this family a break!*

Vincent was polite when responding to questions from Magistrate Kate Thompson, replying "yes, ma'am." Prosecutor Virginia Morgan tendered 16 volumes as the brief of evidence and an index of the brief. Included were a number of receipts from outlets in Leeton. Other items listed included the purchase of a training sword, membership to dating sites, receipts from Mitre 10 in Leeton and the Shell Service Station and a written note by Vincent. Telecommunications records, the purchase of Viagra and a translated Netherlands school report were also included in the brief. Members of the public were disgusted by these revelations. It only confirmed their belief that evil had been walking through the same halls as their children had at Leeton High School; it had been perusing the same aisles as them at local shops and charading as a person who belonged in their small tight-knit community.

In addition to those items, there were also handwriting samples, fingerprints and a forensic procedure consent from Vincent's older brother Luke. The receipts from the Shell Service Station were dated April 3 at 3.21pm and 3.23pm, two days before Stephanie's murder. Another receipt from the Shell Service Station included in the brief was dated April 5—the day of Stephanie's murder—at 10.27pm. The prosecution alleged Stanford murdered Stephanie at Leeton on April 5 between 11am and 7.20pm.

Family members and Stephanie's heartbroken fiancé appeared unable to watch on screen the man accused of murdering their loved one. Vincent was committed to stand trial in the Supreme Court.

\*\*\*

Meanwhile, students and staff at Leeton High School decided to do something Stephanie would love in her honour. It didn't take them long to settle on creating an outdoor amphitheatre in honour of the popular teacher. The school's principal, Greg Horton, said it would be an area the general public, as well as the primary school next door, would be able to utilise too. It would embody everything that Stephanie was—inclusion, with the public invited to use it, performance and fun. Mr Horton said the memorial would be a highlight to a dark year. He said staff had done their best to try and keep things as normal as possible, but that was a herculean task. He said he hoped the amphitheatre would again shine some light on the school, just as Stephanie had done in so many ways.

The slain teacher's family attended the opening of the amphitheatre, where yellow pillars hold the structure together and the back of the stage is adorned with the words "Fly high Steph." It was another emotionally charged day for all who attended. Stephanie's mother said the day marked a new beginning. She paid tribute to her daughter and acknowledged her invaluable contribution as a teacher, colleague and friend. Mrs Scott said her daughter was many things to so many people. She added that Stephanie was dedicated, professional, organised, kind and fair. This last word sent pangs of sadness to all attendees because there was absolutely nothing fair about the way her life had been tragically cut short. Stephanie's mother told the crowd her daughter was a role model, a confidante, a comedian and a fashionista. "She had the ability to laugh at herself and she was able to find and achieve a work/life balance." Mrs Scott shared that it was hard to believe she would never see her beautiful daughter again. "Stephanie has been remembered in so many ways, but this amphitheatre is for you, the students and people of Leeton." Mrs Scott said her daughter would be extremely proud of the way the community had worked together to bring the project to fruition. She fought back tears as she told the people who had come to love her daughter how much her daughter loved being a teacher at Leeton High School. In fact, Stephanie had told her parents that while she was looking forward to her honeymoon, she was also looking forward to returning to school afterwards because she would miss seeing her students every day. They were like family to her and she loved family above all else. Mrs Scott told the students her daughter was watching over them. "She is with you all every day, willing you to succeed in all areas of your lives. Use this amphitheatre to remember Stephanie," she urged those gathered, "to reflect, to laugh, to recall quotes and her wise advice, and to feel her love."

# Chapter Twenty One

The nightmare for the Scott family was far from over. They were forced to endure the horror of hearing—in detail—what had happened to Stephanie while sitting in court. This surely would have been one of the most difficult things they had ever done—particularly with the eyes of everyone else in the courtroom regularly looking their way—but they remained stoic as they always had.

They heard that Stephanie had tried in vain to escape when Vincent accosted her in the school storm room. But his brutish physique had allowed him to simply push her to the floor. Not satisfied that he had total control, he began punching her in the face. Without emotion, he told police he punched her 30 to 40 times.

Stephanie struggled for 40 to 50 seconds before losing consciousness. It was then that Vincent raped Stephanie. When he was finished, he removed a 40-centimetre knife from his pocket and stabbed Stephanie in the neck. He told police he did this to "make sure she was dead."

The details Vincent revealed about his movements following the murder would disgust even the most hardened criminal. He left Stephanie's lifeless body at the school while he returned home to have lunch. Then he returned to the school to clean up.

Stephanie had dropped her car keys as she was being dragged down the corridor by Vincent. He picked them up and drove Stephanie's car into the schoolyard and carried her body to her car. In a bid to stem the bleeding from the wound in her neck he put some yellow masking tape on her neck. He put plastic in the boot of Stephanie's car and put her on top of it. "I put her into the trunk of her car and I got the pressure cleaner out," Vincent said.

For the next few hours, as if in no hurry, he cleaned up the crime scene with the pressure cleaner. He said he then "… drove her car to my house and parked it behind the shed so nobody would see, I went about my day and about 1am Monday morning I went to Cocoparra National Park," he explained.

Prior to going to Cocoparra National Park, Vincent had calmly returned to the school to retrieve his own vehicle. He removed a number of blood-soaked items from the storeroom and loaded them into the back of his ute before leaving.

Vincent also took a number of Stephanie's possessions, including her laptop, which he dumped in a canal outside of Leeton that same afternoon. Before making the trip to Cocoparra National Park, he filled a jerry can with petrol at a Leeton service station. Next, he removed her body from the boot, placed it on the ground and removed her clothes before lighting her on fire. "About 2am I dumped her there [at Cocoparra National Park] and burnt her. I drove back to Pike Road, put her car there and walked home."

When police asked why he had removed her clothing, he told them it was because he was unsure whether they would burn. Vincent left the scene, but not before taking six photographs of Stephanie. Some part of his sick and evil mind told him he might want to revisit the scene—something most people could never imagine in their worst nightmare. Vincent said that he drove Stephanie's car back towards Leeton and dumped it before driving home. However, the judge concluded it was more likely Vincent returned home first to remove the jerry can and plastic before dumping the car. This seems to be a logical conclusion, given the lengthy walk Vincent would have had to return home after leaving the car near Pike Road outside of Leeton.

At about 7.30am Vincent met his mother at a Leeton supermarket and told her he had just been for a walk. His mother told police her son was his usual self and it was normal for him to go on an early morning walk. Vincent said he then returned home and thought he had something to eat before going to bed to sleep for a couple of hours.

# **Chapter Twenty Two**

Later that day, after Vincent awoke, he decided he needed to dispose of the items that belonged to Stephanie he had hidden in his cupboard.

In a brazen act, he drove his ute around Leeton and dumped a number of items of clothing in public garbage bins before driving on to Griffith and dumping more items in bins there. The next morning he rose early as usual for his 4.30am shift at the TAFE educational institution in Leeton.

When Vincent was asked if he had seen Stephanie at Leeton High School on the weekend, he coolly replied he hadn't. In fact, he smiled and even laughed when a colleague remarked the bride-to-be had probably just got cold feet. He actually made light of the catastrophic storm that he had created.

In the early hours of Wednesday morning, between 2am and 3am, Vincent's older brother Luke awoke and went out into the lounge room. He saw Vincent standing near the fireplace. Marcus realized later that Vincent had been burning some of Stephanie's belongings.

Several hours after that Vincent sent a series of text messages to his twin brother Marcus. Vincent asked Marcus what his address was and then sent him a message telling him he was going to send him an envelope. "Keep it safe for me."

Vincent also asked his brother to let him know when he received it. Later that morning, a police officer went to Vincent's home. The cleaner was not home, but Vincent went to the Leeton Police Station about 11am to provide a statement. On this occasion he told police he had been cleaning all weekend. He said the only people he saw at the school had been a number of people roller skating. Vincent had clearly not done his research when coming up with his alibi. His lack of fear of consequences had—thankfully—contributed to his undoing. He told police he had been to the Golden Apple Supermarket on Easter Sunday. This rang an alarm bell to police, who later confirmed this was not true because the supermarket had not opened that day.

When it was later discovered that Vincent had returned to Cocoparra National Park where he had dumped and burnt Stephanie's body, he told police he had done that because he "just wanted to see if she was still there."

On the way back to Leeton he also stopped at the place where he had dumped Stephanie's car. He told police he did this just to have a look as well.

# Chapter Twenty Three

At 6pm on Wednesday, April 8, police returned to Vincent's house to ask him to accompany them to the police station. He was again not home. Police were given permission by Vincent's mother to conduct a walkthrough of the premises. They found fresh tyre tracks leading from the front of the house to a shed in the backyard. Police observed the tracks were left by a vehicle with a smaller wheel base than Vincent's. There was also some yellow tape found near the tracks.

In Vincent's room police found a set of keys that matched the description of those given to Stephanie on Easter Sunday. At this point Vincent's home was declared a crime scene. A short time later Vincent arrived home and told police he had been out taking photos.

It's unclear why he left the set of keys in his room when he had gone to such great lengths to dispose of Stephanie's other possessions. It's also strange that he told police he had been taking photos—surely he should have known this may lead to police asking to look at them.

Police also saw what appeared to be a blood stain on an MDF board (medium density fibreboard, similar to plywood) in the back of Stanford's ute. The dots were all starting to connect—Vincent's attempts to conceal the evidence of the crime had failed spectacularly.

Vincent's ute was seized by police, who discovered a photo of a burnt corpse in bushland on the camera on the passenger seat. When asked, Vincent denied the photo and several others were of Stephanie. Instead, he said he had downloaded the photos from a horror movie because he thought they were funny.

By this time, police knew none of Vincent's explanations were adding up. He was arrested. When asked about the number of scratches on his face and arms he claimed he had bumped his head and ran into a tree branch about a week before. Smears on the MDF board were found to be human blood and a GPS navigation device revealed Vincent had recently searched for Boundary Road, which leads into Cocoparra National Park. This was another tell-tale sign for police. But why didn't Vincent get rid of the GPS?

Perhaps this is something we will never know but it makes you wonder whether Vincent thought he was smarter than the police or whether there was some part of him that wanted to get caught. Police took the cleaner to the police station and gave him the opportunity to speak to a lawyer. On that night he declined to be interviewed but did consent to a number of forensic procedures including photographing of his injuries and the collection of fingernail scrapings, saliva and DNA.

# Chapter Twenty Four

On Thursday, April 9, Stephanie's Mazda 3 was found abandoned at Pike Road in Wamoon, 11 kilometres out of Leeton. On the next day, her burnt remains were found on the edge of Cocoparra National Park. Police quickly ascertained the photos from Vincent's camera had been taken at the scene.

On Saturday, April 11—Stephanie and Aaron's wedding day—Vincent was interviewed and made admissions about the murder.

Police found a number of items at Vincent's home, including the knife used to stab Stephanie and her red bra. Search histories on Vincent's computer and phone showed a pattern of searching for subjects relating to violent rape, violent sex, hard-core pornography and murder. On February 21, for example, he had conducted a number of searches including "bride rape" and "bride kidnapping." The day before Stephanie's murder, Vincent searched terms including "widow maker" and "serial killer knives." Police also discovered that in October the year before Vincent had ordered handcuffs and a half-sword.

On April 13, a forensic pathologist conducted a post mortem examination on Stephanie. Dr Rianie Van Vuuren said the direct cause of death was blunt force head trauma. Stephanie had a small laceration on her right eyebrow, extensive bruising on the right side of her face, a nasal fracture and a "blow-out" fracture of the right eye. Stephanie had two stab wounds on the right side of her neck and she had internal bleeding—on and within the brain.

# Chapter Twenty Five

In October 2016 Stephanie Scott's family and fiancé Aaron Leeson Woolley filed into the Griffith court for a sitting of the NSW Supreme Court. There they would have to face the monster who had taken their beautiful daughter, sister and fiancée. The family maintained a dignified silence throughout the traumatic ordeal. The court heard that Vincent had told police "I think I went a little nuts" when asked why he killed the teacher. "I think I needed to see a psychiatrist but I didn't," he said.

Stephanie's mother Merrilyn bravely addressed the court, asking questions about why Vincent's behaviour was not addressed by his employer. "Within less than a week, he had begun flouting rules and was not challenged," she said. "There were many behaviours that should have raised red flags; his behaviour in the community was also anti-social at best." However, both the Department of Education and the company Vincent worked for denied ever receiving any complaints about his behaviour.

The court heard Vincent was not supposed to have the alarm codes at the school, but he quickly obtained them and would turn the alarm on and off himself.

Mrs Scott said she was haunted by "visions so terrible it is difficult to rest. Did she [Stephanie] see the knife? Did she see the fist before he pounded her precious life into oblivion?"

Mrs Scott told the court that every night she tells Stephanie "goodnight my darling girl."

Vincent avoided her gaze during the hearing, keeping his head down. In her statement, Mrs Scott took aim at the psychopath who had stolen the life of her daughter. "Too pathetic and inept to make a life of his own, he chose to take a life he had no right to," Mrs Scott told the court. She described Vincent as a despicable person, a characterisation no one would dispute.

Mrs Scott bravely shared in court the start of what should have been her speech at Stephanie's wedding. "Now Stephanie and Aaron are starting life together as Mr and Mrs Leeson-Woolley. They will have time to make a history together, little jokes, family holidays, special events and places, their own memories with milestones to celebrate...." she said.

Mrs Scott told the court the wedding speech, like Stephanie's life, would forever remain unfinished. "There were no vows exchanged, no wedding dance performed, no celebration with family and friends."

There were few dry eyes as she told the court Stephanie spent her wedding day alone in the cold sterility of the Griffith morgue. "Instead of enjoying every moment of her evening with loved ones, Stephanie was on the long and lonely journey to meet with the coroner in Glebe," she said. "Her ordeal was coming to a close. Ours was just beginning."

Mrs Scott added that the family's lives had been shattered. "How could this happen to our beautiful girl?"

# Chapter Twenty Six

Defence barrister Janet Manuel conceded Vincent's offences were "without doubt, extremely serious." However, she made a number of submissions she asked the court to consider when sentencing him. She said Vincent's Autism Spectrum Disorder reduced his moral culpability, which would reduce the need for denunciation and general deterrence. "It is recognised, however, that it may also have the effect of making him more of a danger to the community." She also asked to consider his age—24, the fact he accepted responsibility for the crime, and his lack of past criminal convictions.

Crown Prosecutor Lee Carr asked Justice Robert Hulme to jail Vincent for life: "This was a cold-blooded, merciless, sexually motivated killing." Mr Carr said he was asking for the oldest form of justice—not an eye for an eye, but as close as the Australian justice system allowed to this notion—a life for a life.

Justice Hulme said it was plain the case was one of great heinousness. "The offender had harboured violent thoughts, including killing people, since he was a child," he said in his determination. "When he saw Ms Scott his immediate thought was that he had to kill her."

Justice Hulme also said that Vincent had had time to reflect on this urge in the hours that he waited for Stephanie to complete her work at the school, but he persisted with his plan. "Nothing she said or did provided him with a rational motive to do what he did." He added that Ms Scott's only interaction with Vincent was when she wished him a happy Easter.

"On the offender's own account, he beat her a great many times to the head to the point of unconsciousness as he held her to the ground in the darkness of the storage room. He then raped her before bringing out his knife and stabbing her in the neck in order to ensure he had achieved his goal."

Justice Hulme said there were a number of aspects of the offender's confession to police that he could not accept. "The most obvious is his denial of the sexual assault which he now, belatedly, acknowledges." Justice Hulme said it was more concerning that Ms Scott's DNA had been found on a number of items at Vincent's home, including a set of handcuffs. "The offender gave an explanation for this to police—transference of her blood when he put the knife in the wardrobe. That seems an unlikely explanation and its credibility is adversely affected by the fact that he gave it when he was denying the sexual assault."

Justice Hulme said it seemed more likely Vincent had the items at the school at the time of the attack. "That would give rise to the very sinister notion that there was a lot more planning and premeditation than he is prepared to admit," Justice Hulme said. He added the possibility that Ms Scott was Vincent's target before Easter Sunday was further supported by evidence that Vincent searched the term "bride rape" on the internet. "It seems apparent he would not have known that Ms Scott would be at the school on that Easter Sunday. But the matters I have referred to support an inference that he had thought of attacking her before then and when he saw her there that day he saw it as his opportunity and went home to retrieve the various items."

However, Justice Hulme concluded that he believed he should refrain from making such findings beyond reasonable doubt because The Crown did not submit that findings along those lines should be made. "I simply record that I have a very grave concern that the truth has not been fully disclosed and that this was no opportunistic attack upon a target selected at random." Justice Hulme said. He added that a feature that did support the notion there was some type of planning and premeditation was the fact Vincent had a 40 centimetre knife and a condom with him at the school when he claimed he was simply there to clean. "He had them immediately available to him and when he saw Ms Scott his immediate decision was to attack and kill her. I am satisfied of this beyond reasonable doubt and also that he deliberately left the door open to the storage room in order to facilitate the attack when his opportunity arose."

Justice Hulme said the attack involved extreme brutality by a man of substantial size—120 kilograms—upon a defenceless young woman of modest size who had no way to escape or raise the alarm.

Justice Hulme described Vincent's behaviour following the murder as "highly disturbing." "He calmly went home and had a cheese sandwich and a cup of coffee for lunch. He returned to school to clean up the crime scene over several hours and callously loaded Ms Scott's body into the boot of her car."

Justice Hulme also stated that Vincent had carefully planned how to dispose of her body. "Late at night he filled up a jerry can with petrol at a service station, taking care not to drive into the service station itself. He then took the body well away from Leeton to the Cocoparra National Park where he removed all items of clothing, took photographs for some abhorrent reason and then lit a substantial fire to ensure evidence of his sexual depravity was destroyed."

Justice Hulme said he also doubted Vincent had removed Stephanie's clothes at Cocoparra National Park. "Why he removed the clothing and cleaned the body remains only known to him, as does where he did it and what else he did."

Justice Hulme added that Vincent's conniving, callous and self-interested conduct continued when he sent Ms Scott's engagement and graduation rings and her driver's licence to his twin brother Marcus. "Another despicable act was the offender's return to the Cocoparra National Park and photographing the remains. There was also the keeping of Ms Scott's bra as something of a 'souvenir.'"

Justice Hulme said the fact Vincent confessed, along with his mental condition, would usually be taken into account when imposing a sentence. However, he said he was not convinced the offender's moral culpability was reduced due to his Autism Spectrum Disorder. "But even if it was, the extent would be minimal," Justice Hulme said. "The calculating manner in which the offender carried out the various activities following the murder (and to some extent before) indicates that he was well capable of making well-considered choices about how to best serve his own interests and to achieve his objectives."

Justice Hulme stated there was no doubt Vincent was a very disturbed individual. "The evidence concerning his searches on the internet in relation to violent rape; his purchases of knives, handcuffs and other devices capable of use in carrying out acts of extreme violence; his surveillance of the child in his neighbourhood and other such things, together with the assessment, albeit guarded, by Professor Greenberg all indicate to me that the offender will, for a considerable period of time, represent a serious danger to the safety of the community. Whether he will always be so, or whether, as Price J allowed in R v Stani-Reginald, this will moderate with advanced age is difficult to say."

Justice Hulme said, "I am satisfied beyond any doubt that the offender's culpability is so extreme that the community interest in retribution, punishment, community protection and deterrence can only be met with one response."

Vincent was sentenced to 15 years in prison for the rape of Stephanie Scott and life without the possibility of parole for the murder of the loved teacher. There were exclamations of "yes" in the courtroom after the sentences were handed down.

Leeton's Mark Norvall said knowing Vincent would never be back on any street was a great relief. A female newsreader put it aptly that night when reporting on the outcome. "There's a final resolution in what has been a heartbreaking case for Australia and certainly Leeton," she said.

Justice had finally been served.

People again took to social media to share their disbelief at the shocking tragedy. "Reading the court facts at work today was one of the most stomach-turning things I'd seen," wrote one Facebook user.

Another wrote, "I've seen plenty of disgusting things during my time as a reporter but none, none even come close to this. I'm hugging my babies tight tonight, and shedding a tear for all those involved. Love your people hard. Don't let them go."

# Chapter Twenty Seven

No one would dispute that the Scott family had endured more tragedy than any family ever should. Sadly, there was more to come.

In November 2016, Stephanie's father—who had been a tower of strength following her death—died in a freak accident. Mr Scott was working on his property when he was struck and killed by a tree. His death came only weeks after he stood bravely next to his wife as she read her victim impact statement at Vincent Stanford's sentencing.

Mr Scott had retired from his role as a teacher at Canowindra High School at the end of 2015. Principal Neryle Smurthwaite described him as a strong advocate for public education. "It would be remiss not to acknowledge the unparalleled contribution he has made to the young people of our community," she said. "Bob has led the Technological and Applied Studies faculty through significant change and at all times his one focus was on delivering the best education possible for his students whether in the workshop, on the farm or in the classroom.

"Bob, as both head teacher and relieving deputy principal, has been a strong advocate for public education in our community and his determination to forge partnerships between the school and home has been invaluable." He was remembered as a great family man, a great teacher and an even better role model.

Cowra High School teacher Anthony Hamer told *The Canowindra News* that he looked up to Mr Scott as a mentor and for guidance when he first started teaching in the area. "A truly amazing and inspiring man, Mr Bob Scott," Mr Hamer said, "the first male teacher I met as I began my journey here in the Central West and one of the main reasons I stayed in the area in the profession." Mr Hamer said he was thinking of the Scott family. Mr Scott "… changed the lives of so many and he will be sadly missed," he said.

Hundreds of people expressed sadness on social media after hearing of Mr Scott's death. "I guess lots of us from time to time think we have had a tough time or a tough day… and then you think of the Scott family, slowly coming to terms (if ever) with one tragedy and now having to cope with another. My heart breaks for this family," wrote one person on *The Age* website.

"This is so sad. I cried when I first heard it…. I don't know how one family could deal with this much heartache," said another. Noelene Straney said on Facebook that no words could ever ease the family's grief. "Stephanie would have been waiting for him and given him a hug," she said. Jordi Bailey Brown wrote "RIP Mr Scott, one of the best teachers I had at school."

Leeton mayor Paul Maytom said he was saddened to hear of the death of the man whose family had embraced his community after Stephanie's death.

Mr Scott was farewelled at the same funeral venue his daughter was—Eat Your Greens at Eugowra. One of Mr Scott's students recalled how he had a great sense of humour, just like his late daughter. "You always had the lamest jokes that actually made us laugh with how silly they were," Natika Ann said. "You taught us right from wrong. You took everyone under your wing, and made us all a better person. You made high school enjoyable even for those of us who struggled badly. Every time we would see you, you'd always be smiling ear to ear."

Judy Brunby, an attendant at BP in Canowindra, remembered the morning Merrilyn Scott called to order a loaf of bread and milk. Ms Brunby told *The Daily Telegraph* she was more accustomed to hearing Mr Scott's voice on the end of the phone, but his life had tragically been cut short. "Bob was a real gentleman and the town has taken his death badly," she said. "Everyone's feeling for Merrilyn, it's so unfair. She and her family have been through so much tragedy already. When she called to order her bread and milk she sounded normal but she is trying to keep it together for the family."

Canowindra Golf Club greenkeeper John Causins echoed similar sentiments. "We've had a bad run for a little town that used to be about hot air balloons and families," he told *The Daily Telegraph*. "Why is it always the good people who suffer? They are such a loving family."

Mechanic Ken Wilson said Stephanie's death took its toll on Mr Scott, but he soldiered on to ensure he was a rock for his family. "He kept them together and ploughed on, putting his own grief on hold," he said. "He put others first."

What is clear is that the Scott family has endured more than any ever should.

But it's hoped they take some comfort in the fact father and daughter are reunited—in Heaven.

# Chapter Twenty Eight

A week after Mr Scott's tragic death, the Scott family was dealt yet another cruel blow.

It was revealed Vincent had lodged a notice of intention to appeal against his sentence in the Court of Criminal Appeal.

This move angered Leeton's Mark Norvall. "If they kick it out and say it was dealt with properly the first time people will be happy with that," Mr Norvall told *The Sydney Morning Herald*, "but if they give him the right to appeal there will be hell in the land."

Leeton mayor Paul Maytom said news of the appeal was "just terrible timing. It's another blow to the family that is already dealing with something unimaginable in recent days on top of everything else they have been through," he said.

In April 2017, it was revealed Vincent only had three weeks left to lodge an appeal. As the date came to a close, many breathed a sigh of relief but were shocked when it was revealed the callous killer had been given a reprieve. Vincent was gifted a last minute extension to appeal his sentence.

One of Stephanie's former students, Adam Mitchell, condemned the decision. He said this felt like "salt rubbed into a wound. She didn't get a second chance so why should he?" he told Fairfax Media. "Nothing can excuse what he has done and he should never have a chance to do this to somebody else."

An editorial in *The Daily Advertiser* went a long way to capturing how the public felt about news of an appeal. "Through the whole wretched ordeal of their daughter's murder and the subsequent fight for justice, Bob and Merrilyn Scott were unwavering in their stoicism and strength," it read. "In the glare of the national media, they stood as one—poetic when describing their daughter Steph, powerful when describing the impact the murder had on their lives. Just as Steph's authenticity, decency and 'girl next door' relatability resonated with Australians, so too did that of her parents."

The newspaper editorial went on to say that people who had never met the Scotts had been on an emotional journey with them. "So when Mr Scott was killed on Tuesday in a freak accident, the river of tears that had been shed became an ocean. We were left with questions but no answers. What higher force could allow Mrs Scott to lose her daughter to a depraved murderer one year, and lose her husband to an accident the next?"

The editorial said the knowledge that Vincent would be locked in a cage forever would have been a small mercy. "Perversely, just a day after his [Mr Scott's] death, news surfaced of Vincent Stanford signalling an intention to appeal his murder sentence. It marked another slap in the face for a family that had already been hollowed out by tragedy."

The editorial continued by saying that the sheer prospect of Vincent being shown mercy would sit like a shard of glass in the minds of many. "[Vincent] Stanford is a psychopath, a man who stalked Steph like an animal and killed her without a skerrick of conscience or remorse. He deserves to rot in jail, and if such a place as hell exists, to serve an eternal sentence there too."

However, Brett Collins from Justice Action said Vincent had the right to extend his appeal timeframe. "Just because someone happens to be a very unpopular person doesn't mean they should be prevented from having full access to the legal system like everybody else.

"It's not surprising that [Vincent] Stanford would request an extension for his appeal window given he was spending almost all his time alone in a dark room. People in his situation have little to no access to a computer, lawyers and outside consultation so I would argue isolated people need more time."

In early August, there was a collective sigh of relief across Australia when it was revealed Vincent had missed the extended deadline.

Miss Scott's former colleague Sarah Birmingham spoke to Fairfax Media about her "ongoing feeling of unease" knowing that a brutal killer could be given mercy. "He missed the cut off—he's had enough chances and that should be it," she said. "In what bizarre world do we give him yet another chance after what he did? There should be no chance of his release."

# Chapter Twenty Nine

In May 2018, it was revealed the Scott family was seeking further justice. It lodged a claim to sue the NSW government.

The NSW Department of Education was not made aware of the claims filed before proceedings commenced, and a department spokesman declined to comment on the issue. "The department is aware the circumstances resulting in these proceedings are sensitive and all efforts will be made to respond to the claims appropriately," he said in a statement. Stephanie's mother said Stanford was not supposed to have access to the school's alarm codes, but within days he had obtained them and began using them to let himself in and out. He was seen at the school on a number of occasions when he was not supposed to be there. Vincent had been seen lingering around the girls' toilets. Vincent had not been rostered on to work at Leeton High School the day Stephanie was killed.

Fleur Thompson, a spokeswoman for Colin Joss and Co Cleaning, told Fairfax Media if an issue had been raised with the company, it would have been investigated. "Clearly, if we had heard those sort of stories, we would have done something—we had nothing," Ms Thompson said. "If someone had raised a concern, we would have immediately responded and investigated. No one ever raised any concerns. We had no idea."

Ms Thompson claimed that all the mandatory checks for those working with children were done prior to Vincent's employment. "During the six months that he was employed there was no concern raised with us about his behaviour and he completed all his cleaning tasks to the company's standards," she said. "Unfortunately it was unpreventable, correct procedures had been followed." Ms Thompson said the company and its employees were "… in complete shock—you certainly never expect that—especially in a small country town."

Ms Thompson also added that a number of employees at the company were extremely upset about Stephanie's death. "She's always in our thoughts and will never be forgotten. We think about the family too and how difficult times have been for them."

# Chapter Thirty

Almost five years have passed since Stephanie's death sent shockwaves through Leeton. Vincent Stanford will spend the rest of his life at Silverwater Correctional Complex, a men's maximum-security prison outside of Sidney. He mops floors and cleans toilets, earning less than $20 a week.

The murderer, who once giggled when asked if he knew anything about Stephanie Scott's disappearance, has tried to take his own life at least 10 times.

Corrections Minister David Elliott said inmates serving a life sentence for horrendous crimes are now classified as "lifers" because of the risk they posed to the community. "Lifers are responsible for some of the most horrendous crimes in the state and this new classification provides assurance that these inmates will serve out their full and just punishment of life behind barbed wire," Mr Elliott said. "There will no longer be the prospect of any change in their classification and they will always remain in secure confinement to ensure we are keeping the community safe." Lifers cannot be housed in minimum security prisons and their classification cannot ever be reduced. Mr Elliott said the changes would provide certainty for victims and their families about the management of the "worst of the worst."

Even with assurances that Vincent Stanford will never walk the streets again, it does not diminish the loss of Stephanie or that the once innocent town of Leeton, along with small towns everywhere, had been forever changed.

# Chapter Thirty One

"Leeton could not be defined by this tragedy, just as Stephanie's life could not be defined by the terrible manner of her death," Merrilyn shared.

She said in the weeks and months after Stephanie's death, the family was forced to try to return to some sort of normality. "Our children have had to return to work, and this has been difficult for them all," she said. "Stephanie was such a big part of our family, openly confessing her love in her beautifully hand-made cards, offering praise and encouragement. As the weeks and months pass, the darkness persists. In the beginning I would have gladly died, but we have survived, and this pain is a constant in our lives."

She added that "Stephanie is with us during every moment of every day. She is in every activity, in every drawer and cupboard. Her beautiful smile beams out at us from every photo. But we don't need photos. She is in our every cell, a heartbeat away."